dBA… F… WINDOWS FOR DUMMIES™

Quick Reference

by Stuart J. Stuple

IDG BOOKS

IDG Books Worldwide, Inc.
An International Data Group Company

Foster City, CA ♦ Chicago, IL ♦ Indianapolis, IN ♦ Braintree, MA ♦ Dallas, TX

dBASE 5 For Windows For Dummies Quick Reference

Published by
IDG Books Worldwide, Inc.
An International Data Group Company
919 E. Hillsdale Blvd.
Suite 400
Foster City, CA 94404

Library of Congress Catalog Card No.: 94-79603

ISBN 1-56884-953-2

Printed in the United States of America

10 9 8 7 6 5 4 3 2 1

1D/QZ/RS/ZU

Distributed in the United States by IDG Books Worldwide, Inc.

Distributed by Macmillan Canada for Canada; by Computer and Technical Books for the Caribbean Basin; by Contemporanea de Ediciones for Venezuela; by Distribuidora Cuspide for Argentina; by CITEC for Brazil; by Ediciones ZETA S.C.R. Ltda. for Peru; by Editorial Limusa SA for Mexico; by Transworld Publishers Limited in the United Kingdom and Europe; by Al-Maiman Publishers & Distributors for Saudi Arabia; by Simron Pty. Ltd. for South Africa; by IDG Communications (HK) Ltd. for Hong Kong; by Toppan Company Ltd. for Japan; by Addison Wesley Publishing Company for Korea; by Longman Singapore Publishers Ltd. for Singapore, Malaysia, Thailand and Indonesia; by Unalis Corporation for Taiwan; by WS Computer Publishing Company, Inc. for the Philippines; by WoodsLane Pty. Ltd. for Australia; by WoodsLane Enterprises Ltd. for New Zealand.

For general information on IDG Books in the U.S., including information on discounts and premiums, contact IDG Books at 800-434-3422 or 415-655-3000.

For information on where to purchase IDG Books outside the U.S., contact IDG Books International at 415-655-3021 or fax 415-655-3295.

For information on translations, contact Marc Jeffrey Mikulich, Director, Foreign & Subsidiary Rights, at IDG Books Worldwide, 415-655-3018 or fax 415-655-3295.

For sales inquiries and special prices for bulk quantities, write to the address above or call IDG Books Worldwide at 415-655-3000.

For information on using IDG Books in the classroom, or ordering examination copies, contact Jim Kelly at 800-434-2086.

IDG
BOOKS

About the Author

Stuart J. Stuple has worked with computers since back when they were gasoline powered. (OK, it hasn't been that long, but it feels like it.) He spends most of his days playing with new software, wishing he had better hardware, and trying to decide between using his Macintosh or his Windows machine for whatever project he is working on. He started out as a computer book editor and project manager many years ago, but his spelling is so bad they made him an author instead. He has a Master of Arts in Counseling Psychology, which helps him deal with the joys of writing. In addition, Stuart has worked as a full-time Computer Science instructor in community colleges in both California and Washington. The last several months have been spent writing the *Quattro Pro For Dummies Quick Reference*, the *System 7.5 For Dummies Quick Reference*, and this delightful book you are now holding; while writing them, he was wishing he could go outside.

ABOUT IDG BOOKS WORLDWIDE

VIII
WINNER
Eighth Annual Computer Press Awards 1992

IX
WINNER
Ninth Annual Computer Press Awards 1993

IDG BOOKS

Welcome to the world of IDG Books Worldwide.

IDG Books Worldwide, Inc. is a subsidiary of International Data Group, the world's largest publisher of computer-related information and the leading global provider of information services on information technology. IDG was founded more than 25 years ago and now employs more than 7,000 people worldwide. IDG publishes more than 220 computer publications in 65 countries (see listing below). More than fifty million people read one or more IDG publications each month.

Launched in 1990, IDG Books Worldwide is today the #1 publisher of best-selling computer books in the United States. We are proud to have received 3 awards from the Computer Press Association in recognition of editorial excellence, and our best-selling *...For Dummies*™ series has more than 12 million copies in print with translations in 25 languages. IDG Books, through a recent joint venture with IDG's Hi-Tech Beijing, became the first U.S. publisher to publish a computer book in the People's Republic of China. In record time, IDG Books has become the first choice for millions of readers around the world who want to learn how to better manage their businesses.

Our mission is simple: Every IDG book is designed to bring extra value and skill-building instructions to the reader. Our books are written by experts who understand and care about our readers. The knowledge base of our editorial staff comes from years of experience in publishing, education, and journalism — experience which we use to produce books for the '90s. In short, we care about books, so we attract the best people. We devote special attention to details such as audience, interior design, use of icons, and illustrations. And because we use an efficient process of authoring, editing, and desktop publishing our books electronically, we can spend more time ensuring superior content and spend less time on the technicalities of making books.

You can count on our commitment to deliver high-quality books at competitive prices on topics consumers want to read about. At IDG, we value quality, and we have been delivering quality for more than 25 years. You'll find no better book on a subject than an IDG book.

John Kilcullen
President and CEO
IDG Books Worldwide, Inc.

IDG Books Worldwide, Inc. is a subsidiary of International Data Group, the world's largest publisher of computer-related information and the leading global provider of information services on information technology. International Data Group publishes over 220 computer publications in 65 countries. More than fifty million people read one or more International Data Group publications each month. The officers are Patrick J. McGovern, Founder and Board Chairman; Kelly Conlin, President; Jim Casella, Chief Operating Officer. International Data Group's publications include: ARGENTINA'S Computerworld Argentina, Infoworld Argentina; AUSTRALIA'S Computerworld Australia, Computer Living, Australian PC World, Australian Macworld, Network World, Mobile Business Australia, Publish!, Reseller, IDG Sources; AUSTRIA'S Computerwelt Oesterreich, PC Test; BELGIUM'S Data News (CW); BOLIVIA'S Computerworld; BRAZIL'S Computerworld, Connections, Game Power, Mundo Unix, PC World, Publish, Super Game; BULGARIA'S Computerworld Bulgaria, PC & Mac World Bulgaria, Network World Bulgaria; CANADA'S CIO Canada, Computerworld Canada, InfoCanada, Network World Canada, Reseller; CHILE'S Computerworld Chile, Informatica; COLOMBIA'S Computerworld Colombia, PC World; COSTA RICA'S PC World; CZECH REPUBLIC'S Computerworld, Elektronika, PC World; DENMARK'S Communications World, Computerworld Danmark, Computerworld Focus, Macintosh Produktkatalog, Macworld Danmark, PC World Danmark, PC Produktguide, Tech World, Windows World; ECUADOR'S PC World Ecuador; EGYPT'S Computerworld (CW) Middle East, PC World Middle East; FINLAND'S MikroPC, Tietoviikko, Tietoverkko; FRANCE'S Distributique, GOLDEN MAC, InfoPC, Le Guide du Monde Informatique, Le Monde Informatique, Telecoms & Reseaux; GERMANY'S Computerwoche, Computerwoche Focus, Computerwoche Extra, Electronic Entertainment, Gamepro, Information Management, Macwelt, Netzwelt, PC Welt, Publish, Publish; GREECE'S Publish & Macworld; HONG KONG'S Computerworld Hong Kong, PC World Hong Kong; HUNGARY'S Computerworld SZT, PC World; INDIA'S Computers & Communications; INDONESIA'S Info Komputer; IRELAND'S ComputerScope; ISRAEL'S Beyond Windows, Computerworld Israel, Multimedia, PC World Israel; ITALY'S Computerworld Italia, Lotus Magazine, Macworld Italia, Networking Italia, PC Shopping Italy, PC World Italia; JAPAN'S Computerworld Today, Information Systems World, Macworld Japan, Nikkei Personal Computing, SunWorld Japan, Windows World; KENYA'S East African Computer News; KOREA'S Computerworld Korea, Macworld Korea, PC World Korea; LATIN AMERICA'S GamePro; MALAYSIA'S Computerworld Malaysia, PC World Malaysia; MEXICO'S Compu Edicion, Compu Manufactura, Computacion/Punto de Venta, Computerworld Mexico, MacWorld, Mundo Unix, PC World, Windows; THE NETHERLANDS' Computer! Totaal, Computable (CW), LAN Magazine, Lotus Magazine, MacWorld; NEW ZEALAND'S Computer Buyer, Computerworld New Zealand, Network World, New Zealand PC World; NIGERIA'S PC World Africa; NORWAY'S Computerworld Norge, Lotusworld Norge, Macworld Norge, Maxi Data, Networld, PC World Ekspress, PC World Nettverk, PC World Norge, PC World's Produktguide, Publish& Multimedia World, Student Data, Unix World, Windowsworld; PAKISTAN'S PC World Pakistan; PANAMA'S PC World Panama; PERU'S Computerworld Peru, PC World; PEOPLE'S REPUBLIC OF CHINA'S China Computerworld, China Infoworld, China PC Info Magazine, Computer Fan, PC World China, Electronics International, Electronics Today/Multimedia World, Electronic Product World, China Network World, Software World Magazine, Telecom Product World, PHILIPPINES' Computerworld Philippines, PC Digest (PCW); POLAND'S Computerworld Poland, Computerworld Special Report, Networld, PC World/Komputer, Sunworld; PORTUGAL'S Cerebro/PC World, Correio Informatico/Computerworld, MacIn; ROMANIA'S Computerworld, PC World, Telecom Romania; RUSSIA'S Computerworld-Moscow, Mir - PK (PCW), Sety (Networks); SINGAPORE'S Computerworld Southeast Asia, PC World Singapore; SLOVENIA'S Monitor Magazine; SOUTH AFRICA'S Computer Mail (CIO),Computing S.A.,Network World S.A., Software World; SPAIN'S Advanced Systems, Amiga World, Computerworld Espana, Communicaciones World, Macworld Espana, NeXTWORLD, Super Juegos Magazine (GamePro), PC World Espana, Publish; SWEDEN'S Attack, ComputerSweden, Corporate Computing, Macworld, Mikrodatorn, Natverk & Kommunikation, PC World, CAP & Design, DataIngenjoren, Maxi Data,Windows World; SWITZERLAND'S Computerworld Schweiz, Macworld Schweiz, PC Tip; TAIWAN'S Computerworld Taiwan, PC World Taiwan; THAILAND'S Thai Computerworld; TURKEY'S Computerworld Monitor, Macworld Turkiye, PC World Turkiye; UKRAINE'S Computerworld, Computers+Software Magazine; UNITED KINGDOM'S Computing /Computerworld, Connexion/Network World, Lotus Magazine, Macworld, Open Computing/Sunworld; URAGUAY'S PC World Uraguay; UNITED STATES' Advanced Systems, AmigaWorld, Cable in the Classroom, CD Review, CIO, Computerworld, Computerworld Client/Server Journal, Digital Video, DOS World, Electronic Entertainment Magazine (E2), Federal Computer Week, Game Hits, GamePro, IDG Books, Infoworld, Laser Event, Macworld, Maximize, Multimedia World, Network World, PC Letter, PC World, Publish, SWATPro, Video Event; VENEZUELA'S Computerworld Venezuela, PC World; VIETNAM'S PC World Vietnam. 11-16-94

Credits

Executive Vice President, Strategic Planning and Research
David Solomon

Editorial Director
Diane Graves Steele

Acquisitions Editor
Megg Bonar

Brand Manager
Judith A. Taylor

Editorial Managers
Tracy L. Barr
Sandra Blackthorn

Editorial Assistants
Tamara S. Castleman
Stacey Holden Prince
Kevin Spencer

Acquisitions Assistant
Suki Gear

Production Director
Beth Jenkins

Associate Project Coordinator
Valery Bourke

Pre-Press Coordinator
Steve Peake

Project Editor
Kathleen M. Cox

Editor
Diane L. Giangrossi

Technical Reviewer
Gordon S. Cooper

Production Staff
Paul Belcastro
Mark Owens
Carla Radzakinas
Dwight Ramsey
Patricia R. Reynolds
Gina Scott
Kathie Schnorr

Proofreader
Henry Lazarek

Indexer
Anne Leach

Book Design
University Graphics

Cover Design
Kavish + Kavish

Acknowledgments

On a personal note (A♭ I believe), I'd like to thank Bjoern and Erynn who put up with all of the neeping. For those who don't recognize the word, *to neep* is the specialized term for carrying on conversations using so many specialized words that no one else can understand you. Nerds neep. Science fiction junkies neep. Celtic and Norse scholars neep, but they pronounce it oddly.

Then there are all the wonderful people who help actually turn my writing into a book. Kathy Cox deserves the credit for managing this project (and the author). Not only did she do a great job, but she let me come up with the secret code phrase for identifying my phone calls. Gordon Cooper put up with my attitude and checked the entire manuscript for technical accuracy. Thanks to both for the support and the editing. Diane Giangrossi was responsible for translating my material into English. Although they call it *copy editing*, in my case, it's sometimes much closer to archaeological work on a dead language. By the way, all of these deserve the thanks for correcting many of my mistakes. I deserve any blame for any that may remain.

I'd also like thank Diane Steele for giving me direction and encouragement (not to mention new projects). Likewise, Mary Bednarek has my thanks and my friendship for always getting in touch just when I need a little boost in my day. Megg Bonar and Suki Gear put up with weekly panic calls and make sure that my checks get signed. For that, I thank you, my bank thanks you, and all my creditors thank you.

Finally, I'd like to thank the people who take the final manuscript and turn it into a real book. That includes everybody in production, but for this book Valery Bourke in particular. As long as I never hear the 75% calculation again, I'll be a happy man. Also, Henry Lazarek had the thankless task of proofreading the actual book, and anyone who can pay attention to that many details has to be outstanding. And besides, it's not really thankless because I thank you. Finally, Anne Leach deserves a special thanks if you can find anything in this book — she compiled the index.

(The Publisher would like to give special thanks to Patrick J. McGovern, without whom this book would not have been possible.)

Contents at a Glance

Introduction

Introduction

Welcome to the wonderful world of dBASE for Windows. This book, the *dBASE 5 For Windows For Dummies Quick Reference*, is your personal guide to all of the features you'll need to learn within the dBASE universe. I've covered each and every command that you are likely to encounter — explaining not only how to use the command itself, but providing shortcuts and tips so that you can use it more effectively and efficiently. Almost more importantly, I've made an effort to exclude those commands that you won't need to master — those associated with creating your own programs or procedures. In addition to dBASE, you probably are also using Crystal Reports, which is the separate program used to create labels, reports, and cross-tabs, but that's a different story and a different book.

In the Command Reference section, you'll find an alphabetical list of all of the commands used within dBASE for working with data tables, creating forms and queries, printing and previewing reports and labels, as well as customizing the properties of the dBASE environment. Each command is listed by the menu name followed by the command name. In other words, the Print command from the File menu can be found under File⇨Print. For each command, I've given a brief description, listed each and every shortcut for the command, provided you with the basics that you need to use the command, and then have given you the benefit of my wisdom with notes, tips, and warnings. In addition, each command is cross-referenced to other commands within the quick reference and to examples and further explanations in Scott Palmer's *dBASE For Windows For Dummies*.

Following the Command Reference is Stuart's Superior SpeedBar Survey, which shows each of the major SpeedBars in the dBASE environment, explains each button on the SpeedBar, and tells you which command to check for more on using the button. For those of you not familiar with Borland's terms for things, a SpeedBar is a set of buttons located below the menu bar. Each button represents a different command. In many programs, the term *toolbar* is used to refer to the same thing.

The last two items in the book are perhaps the most important. The Glossary provides definitions for many of the unfamiliar words you may encounter while working with dBASE. In addition, it's where I buried some of my best jokes. Finally, the Index provides you with another way of finding things. If you don't know the command you need, try checking the Index for an entry about what you are trying to do. Of course, if you do know the command, you can just look it up in the Command Reference — remember, it's alphabetical.

What Do These Pesky Icons Mean?

Oh, one more thing. This book is filled with funny little pictures designed to make comprehension a little easier. These pictures are called icons. The following list tells you what each stands for.

This icon flags commands that are recommended for the average dBASE 5 for Windows user.

This icon points out commands that are not recommended for the average dBASE 5 for Windows user

This icon designates the kind of command that an average dBASE 5 for Windows user may not want to use, but learning this command could come in handy.

This icon flags commands that you can safely use.

This icon flags commands that are usually safe, but if you're not careful, you may run into trouble.

This icon designates commands that pose some danger to your data if you don't use them correctly, so be careful. You may be better off having someone else use these commands for you.

This icon points out commands that you should never use unless you're some kind of programmer or technical guru.

This icon points out a command that involves both your dBASE 5 for Windows program and your Crystal Reports program. Most of these commands open Crystal Reports, where you have an entirely different universe of commands. Unfortunately, I wasn't able to cover both Crystal Reports and dBASE 5 for Windows in this Quick Reference.

This icon warns of problem areas and potentially dangerous situations.

This icon flags helpful information that will make life with dBASE 5 for Windows easier.

This icon indicates a cross reference to another entry or section within this Quick Reference.

This icon flags cross-references to material in IDG's *dBASE For Windows For Dummies* book.

Part I

Command Reference

Catalog⇨Add Item

Puts an item, such as a database table, form, or report, into the current catalog — which is a very good place for it. A catalog allows you to group items for easy access (whoops, that's the other Windows database program).

For keyboard krazies

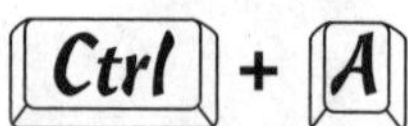

For mouse maniacs

This button is only available when you're in a catalog (which is fine, because that's the only time you can add an item to a catalog).

Just the facts

First, open the catalog in which you are going to put the item, if that catalog isn't active already. (You can tell which catalog is active by looking at the icon to the left of the title: an open book indicates an active catalog.) Then you need to locate the file containing the item. Start by selecting Catalog⇨Add Item (or the keyboard or mouse shortcut). Use the File Types list at the bottom of the Add Catalog Item dialog box to choose what types of files to list; then use the Directory and Drive boxes at the right to move among your files. Once you locate the file that contains the information you wish to add, double-click it (or just click it once and select OK).

You can provide a short description of the item in the Catalog Item Description dialog box that comes up. Putting down a description is a very good idea, as it allows you to recognize the various parts of your catalog later. After all, those short, eight-letter names can get rather cryptic.

More stuff

You can also add an item to a catalog by dragging it from another catalog window or from the Navigator. If you try to add a table while viewing your forms, dBASE is usually smart enough to make sure that the table is displayed in the proper group — that the table is added to the table list, not the forms list. Of course, even dBASE makes mistakes: in the sample files that ship with the program, a DBF (table) is listed with the queries for the EQUIPMNT catalog.

If you want to add a new item to a catalog, you can either use File⇨New, or you can select the untitled file that represents that type of item and then select the appropriate New command from the Catalog menu. Each type of item has its own command that only appears when the untitled file for that type is selected. For example, to create a new Form, set the catalog to display forms (View⇨Forms) and click the untitled form file. Then select Catalog⇨New Form. If you're viewing reports instead and select the untitled report, the command is Catalog⇨New Report.

Organizing your database files into catalogs makes them much easier to locate and to work with. Each catalog should only contain files that are somehow related to a similar project. A single file (or item) can belong to several different catalogs. Be somewhat careful with this technique because any changes to the file will show up in all the catalogs to which it belongs.

If you use a database table or a query as the basis for a report or form, the table or query is automatically added to the active catalog.

For a detailed explanation of putting things into catalogs, see Chapter 4 of *dBASE For Windows For Dummies*.

To remove an item, use Edit⇨Delete. To change the description of an item in a catalog, use Properties⇨Selected Catalog Item. (If you're working in the Navigator, the command is Properties⇨Selected File Item.)

Catalog⇨Add Records

Opens the selected table so that you can add new records to the end of the file using the default form view. You have to select a table in a catalog before using this command.

Just the facts

Select the table you want to work with and then select Catalog⇨Add Records. Enter your information in the blank form that comes up. Use the arrow keys or Tab or Enter to move between the fields. When you are in the last field on the form and press Enter or Tab, the record you have been working with is saved and you are taken to a new blank form. When you finish adding records, you can close the table or move on to any other command.

More stuff

If you'd rather, you can move to the last field in the last record in the table and press Tab or Enter. When you do, you get a dialog box asking you whether to add records. Select Yes and you can add as many as you'd like.

To add records in the columnar view, use Catalog⇨Edit Records. Actually, you can control which view you use with Catalog⇨Add Records and Catalog⇨Edit Records by using the Files category of Properties⇨Desktop. Use the commands at the bottom of the Table menu (such as Table⇨Next Record and Table⇨Previous Record) to move between records.

Catalog⇨Debug

Opens the dBASE Debugger, which is a separate program you can use to check for errors in programs or applications that you have created using dBASE for Windows. Use this command only if you own a different pocket protector for each day of the week and live off Twinkies and Cheetos. In other words, this is a nerds-only command and not a topic discussed in front of a proper audience.

Catalog⇨Design Form

Opens the selected form so that you can make changes to its design — that is, what's on the form, how the form looks, and how you move between items on the form. Of course, to get to the command, you have to first select a form within the current catalog.

For keyboard krazies

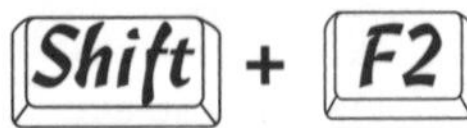

For mouse maniacs

This button is used to open the selected item so that you can make changes to its design.

Just the facts

All you need to do is select the form you want to work with and then select Catalog⇨Design Form. The selected form is opened in the Form Designer, and your screen fills with all the tools available for changing what's on the form as well as how the form looks and is organized. For information about creating a new form, see Catalog⇨New Form.

If you don't have anything on your form yet, you need to add something using the Controls window shown here. (To display the Controls window, try to find the Controls entry on the Window menu. If it's not there, use View⇨Controls.) Be warned that each of the controls serves a very different purpose, and the details of using each type are much more than I can deal with in the pages they give me. Some of the controls are more appropriate for working with forms that are used to enter data into the database (called *input forms*), and others are used primarily with forms that just display information. Fortunately, designing the form is the same no matter what purpose it will serve.

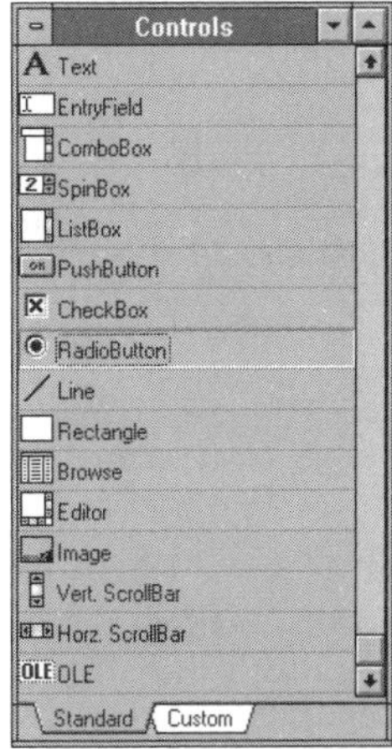

To create a control on your form, click on the type of control you want from the Controls window and then use your mouse to draw the outline of the control on your form. Position the mouse where one corner of the control is to go, and hold down the left mouse button while dragging to the opposite corner. One of the most common controls is the EntryField, which is just a blank text box. Also very popular for designing input forms are the ComboBox and the ListBox. Both of these give you a list of items to choose from. Although the ListBox always displays your choices, the ComboBox list drops down only when you click the control. The all-time favorite control is probably the TextBox, which is used to add labels or background text to your form. To delete a control, select it and select Edit⇨Delete.

Of course, the odds are good that you aren't particularly happy with just throwing controls onto a gray background. If you're like most people, you want more control. Well, far be it from me to deny you what you want; the power is yours. To change the look and functioning of a control, select the control by clicking it once and then move to the Properties window. If the Properties window is showing on your screen, you can just click it. If it's not showing, check the Window menu. If it's listed there, select it. Finally, if the Properties window is not listed on the Window menu, select View⇨Object Properties. You only need to do this the first time you use the Properties window while working with a particular form; after that, it's added to the Window menu. The choices on a Properties window change, depending on what type of control you have selected, but the window will look something like the one shown here.

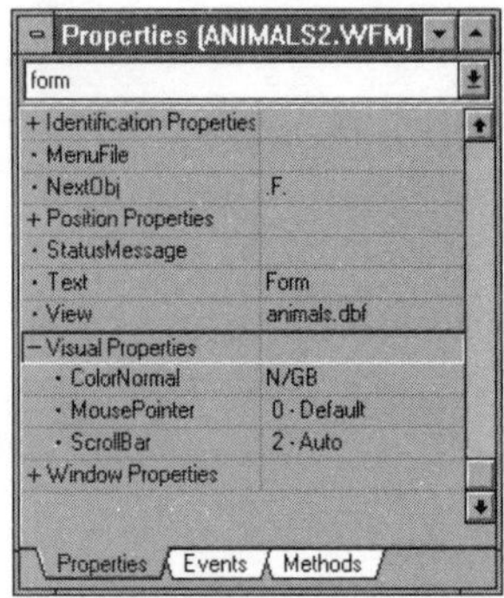

Entries with a plus next to them contain subcategories of information that can be displayed by double-clicking the entry. Entries with a small dot do not have subcategories, and entries with a minus sign have subcategories that are already being displayed. Double-click the minus sign to collapse the list of subcategories.

The Properties window has two columns: The one on the left lists the properties; the one on the right lists the values for those properties. To change a property, click the box in the right column and enter the new value. Some properties offer a drop-down list of choices. (If a small down-arrow appears to the right of the box after you click it, that means there's a drop-down list.) Other properties — such as the name of the control or the label to be displayed with the control — require you to enter the proper value from the keyboard. Finally, some controls have a builder tool to help you fill in the proper value. These controls are identified by a small button on the right with an image of a wrench. Click the wrench for a dialog box that offers tools for selecting the value for the properties. For example, the dialog box shown here is the builder tool for selecting a color.

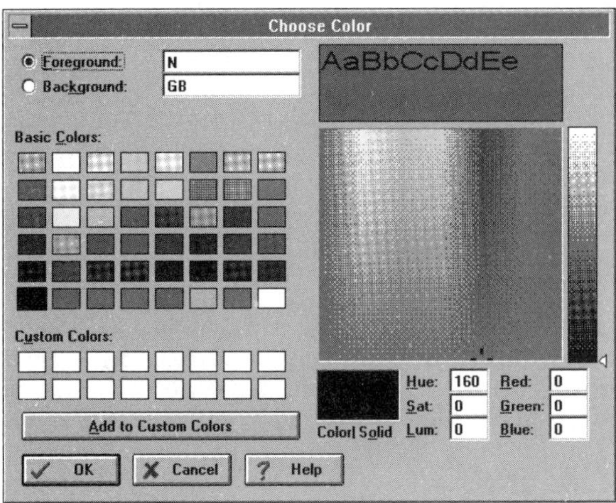

Many properties determine the look of the control, including the Font Properties, Position Properties, and Visual Properties. You can use these properties along with the commands on the Layout menu to make your form more attractive and easier to use. You can also use the mouse to move a control or to change a control's size. To move the control, place your cursor within the control and drag to the new location. To change a field's size, select the field by clicking it and then drag one of the eight handles (small, black squares) around the border of the field. Drag a side handle to adjust a single side and a corner handle to move the two adjacent sides.

Other properties determine how the control works. The most important of these is the DataLink property, which associates the control with a field in one of your database tables. Each form can only be associated with a single table, but you can place a subform control onto any form. The subform can then be associated with a different table. Anyway, the DataLink property is one property where you generally use the builder. The first time you click the wrench button, you are presented with a dialog box for selecting the table to associate with the form. After that, you are given a list of all the fields in the form. To associate a control with a particular field, simply select the field you want to use. The DataLink value changes to the name of the database table, an arrow symbol, and the name of the field. Now when you use the form, the entries for the associated field are displayed in the control.

I mentioned that two of the most common controls for input forms are the ComboBox and the ListBox. Both of these have a special property that is used to create the list of values displayed by the control. This property, DataSource, is found in the Data Linkage Properties group along with the DataLink property and is used to select the source of the list. The most common choice is usually Field, which displays all the values that have already been assigned to that field. The final choice in the Data Linkage Properties group is Sorted, which determines how the entries in the list are organized.

This is just enough information to get you started. You'll find that building a form that works for you is part learning how to use the various commands and tools and part a matter of style. Some people like their forms arranged with the controls placed close together and in shades of gray. Others prefer the controls scattered around the form and in a variety of bright colors. The best way to learn is to experiment. Use View⇨Form to actually see how your form looks and behaves.

More stuff

When you are done changing the properties for a control, don't close the Properties window. Instead, use the Window menu to move back to your form (or, if part of the form is visible, simply click on the form itself). Also, if you want to change the properties for more than one control, you can use the drop-down list at the top of the Properties window to choose between the controls on the form.

When you open a form to change its design, dBASE must be able to locate all the files associated with the form. This means that if you add a form to a new catalog, the first time you open the form to work with the design, all the associated files are also added to the catalog for you.

To learn more about customizing a form, see Chapter 14 in *dBASE For Windows For Dummies*.

If you just want to use a form, you can double-click on the form or select the form and then select Catalog⇨Run Form. If you are working with a form and want to switch to Design view for that form, select View⇨Form Design. Use View⇨Order View to control how pressing Tab moves you through your form.

Catalog⇨Design Labels

Opens the selected file of labels so that you can make changes. Although you can print the labels from within dBASE, as soon as you start to work with the label's design, you are switched into Crystal Reports. To even find the Catalog⇨Design Labels command, you must first select a file of labels in the current catalog.

For keyboard krazies

For mouse maniacs

This button opens the selected item so you can change the design. With a label, that means that you're opening Crystal Reports.

Just the facts

After you select the set of labels you want to change, select Catalog⇨Design Labels (or one of the shortcuts), and the description for the set of labels is loaded into Crystal Reports. You can change the physical arrangement of the labels on the page by using File⇨Set Label Layout (a Crystal Reports command not covered here), and you can use any of the Crystal Reports commands to make changes to the layout of the label. For more on designing labels, see Catalog⇨New Labels.

More stuff

To use the label file, use Catalog⇨Run Labels.

Catalog⇨Design Program

This isn't something you want to be doing, so I'm not going to tell you about it. After all, some people earn their livings by writing dBASE programs, and you should do your bit for the economy by hiring one of them. Besides, writing programs is very nerdy and not much fun.

Catalog⇨Design Query

Opens the selected query in design view so that you can make changes to the request. You can change which fields are displayed in the resulting table as well as what values are used when matching records. To get to this command, first select a query in the current catalog.

For keyboard krazies

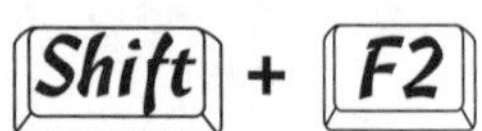

For mouse maniacs

With a query selected, this button opens the query so that you can make changes.

Just the facts

To open a query in Design view, simply select the query item by clicking it once and then select Catalog⇨Design Query. The steps for making changes to a query are based on these same concepts and use the same tools as designing a new query. For more information, see Catalog⇨New Query.

More stuff

To view the results of the query, you can either double-click the query item or select the query and then select Catalog⇨Run Query. If you've already opened a query to work with, you can move to the design view by selecting View⇨Query Design. To see the results of the query, use View⇨Query Results.

Catalog⇨Design Report

Opens Crystal Reports with the selected report already loaded and ready for changing. The command is only available if you have selected a report in the current catalog. You use the same command whether the report is organized as columns or as a cross-tab.

For keyboard krazies

For mouse maniacs

This button opens Crystal Reports with the selected report so that you can make changes.

Just the facts

Click once on the report you want to change and then select Catalog⇨Design Report. Now you're in Crystal Reports, where you can make whatever changes you wish. For more information about the tools that are available, see Catalog⇨New Report.

More stuff

If all you want to do is print the report, you can stay within dBASE and not bother with Crystal Reports. Just select the report and use the Catalog⇨Run Report command. A preview of the report appears. Use File⇨Print to print the report. For greater control, you need to open the report in Crystal Reports.

For information about controlling which records are shown in the report, you need to modify the query used by the report with Catalog⇨Design Query. For more information about working with queries, see Catalog⇨New Query.

Catalog⇨Design Table Structure

Displays the list of fields that make up the selected table's structure. You can adjust the table by changing field definitions, rearranging fields, and adding or removing fields.

For keyboard krazies

For mouse maniacs

With a table selected, this command gives you access to the table's structure so that you can make changes to the actual fields (rather than to their contents).

Just the facts

Select the table you want to modify and then select Catalog⇨Design Table Structure. The basic techniques are the same as those you used when creating the table (see Catalog⇨New Table), but with one important difference: your table may now have information in it. If you delete a field, you lose all the information that was in that field. Furthermore, if you change the field's type or shorten the field, you may lose part of the information. In short, be very careful when making changes to the structure of an existing table.

More stuff

To find out how to change the table structure, or about special formatting for fields, see Chapter 8 in *dBASE For Windows For Dummies*.

To move from viewing the contents of a table to working with the Design, use View⇨Table Records. If you want to work with the records in a table, use Catalog⇨Edit Records. To add new records to a table, use Catalog⇨Add Records.

Catalog⇨Do

Runs the selected program. Hopefully, the program was written for you by someone else and does exactly what you want it to. If you have to write your own programs, you're beyond what's covered in this book. Good luck!

Catalog⇨Edit as Program

dBASE offers two methods for viewing forms and queries: the nice tools on-screen or a bunch of cryptic text commands. Catalog⇨Edit as Program shows you the cryptic text commands that make up the actual program used for the form or query, whereas, using the designer, Catalog⇨Design Form shows you the form itself and lets you make changes, and Catalog⇨Design Query shows you a screen where you can define your query using your mouse. Both methods give you the same information, but seeing the objects rather than the programming code makes the information much easier to understand. Be smart and take the easy way out: Don't use Catalog⇨Edit as Program.

Catalog⇨Edit Records

Opens the selected table and displays the records contained in the table so that you can make changes to the contents. This is the command you use to change the information stored in your database.

For keyboard krazies

For mouse maniacs

This button opens the selected table so that you can change the contents of the fields.

Just the facts

Select the table that contains the information you want to change and then select Catalog⇨Edit Records. You can then use the arrow keys or the mouse to move between the various records and fields until you find the information you want to change. You can press F2 to change between the various views of your data (View⇨Browse Layout, View⇨Columnar Layout, and View⇨Form Layout).

Once you're in the cell where you want to make changes, you have a couple of choices. If you want to replace everything in the cell, you can just start typing the new information. If you want to make changes to what's already there rather than replace it, use the mouse or arrow keys to position your cursor. Any characters you type are inserted at the cursor and you can use either Delete or Backspace to remove characters. When the cell contains the information you want, simply move to a new location (by pressing Enter or Tab, clicking with the mouse, or following whatever technique suits your fancy at the moment).

More stuff

If all you want to do is add some new records, use CatalogÍAdd Records.

Catalog⇨New Cross-Tab

Creates a new report in Crystal Reports, organized so that the information for two or more overlapping groups is summarized. Two groups overlap when there are records for many, if not all, of the possible combinations. One group might have colors (Red, Green, and Blue) and the other shapes (Squares, Triangles, and Circles). The groups overlap if most of the combinations exist as records (Red Squares, Red Triangles, Red Circles, Green Squares, Green Triangles, and so on). A cross-tab report summarizes a value in a third field (such as number of pieces) for each possible combination of the two groups. Although you can use the cross-tab format with one group or even with none, in those cases it's better to use Catalog⇨New Report.

Just the facts

The first thing you need to do is make sure that the data in your table is going to work with a cross-tab report. You need to have at least two overlapping groups. For example, you may need to summarize the number of bulbs planted for each color for various types of flowers. The various colors and the types of flowers make your two overlapping groups. Each of the three colors (red, white, and yellow) and each of the three types of flowers (roses, tulips, and dahlias) are combined to create nine entries (red roses, red tulips, red dahlias, white roses, white tulips, white dahlias, yellow roses, yellow tulips, and yellow dahlias). OK, you probably won't ever need to do this, but it's my example and I'm going on with it. The information in the database looks something like the table shown here.

Table Records (FLOWERS.DBF)

Rec	TYPE	COLOR	NO_BULBS	YR_PLANTE
8	Carnations	Red	82	1992
9	Carnations	White	219	1992
10	Carnations	Pink	57	1992
18	Carnations	Red	103	1993
19	Carnations	White	194	1993
20	Carnations	Pink	93	1992
1	Roses	Red	154	1992
2	Roses	White	127	1992
3	Roses	Yellow	98	1992
4	Roses	Pink	119	1992
11	Roses	Red	168	1993

A cross-tab report would be organized with three columns (perhaps one for each color) and three rows (one for each type of flower), and the summary value for each entry would fit neatly into one of the boxes. Why, gosh, there's a cross-tab report right here using the information I just showed you. Isn't it great the way they organize these books?

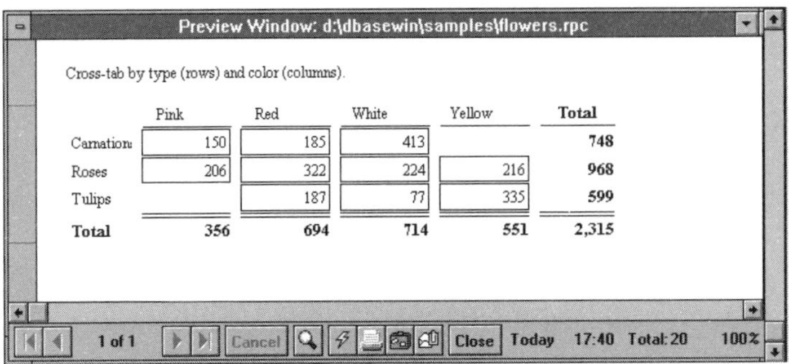

Of course, what you probably want to know is how to get from Picture A (the data) to Picture B (the report). Well, I'll tell you. First, select Catalog⇨New Cross-Tab (or any of the similar commands, such as Navigator⇨New Cross-Tab, or File⇨New⇨Cross-Tab). Now you're in Crystal Reports (which is where you actually create the cross-tab). Depending on what you did last, you may be immediately asked to select a database file, or you may be in the Cross-Tab dialog box with a database already selected. If the Cross-Tab dialog box shows up with the database you want to use, you can just skip the next paragraph (lucky you).

If you weren't so lucky, you need to locate the database or query you want to use for the report. If the Cross-Tab dialog box is displayed but the database listed isn't the one you want to use, you need to click the Cancel button and then use File⇨New⇨Cross-Tab (within Crystal Reports) to start over. If you've started over or if the Cross-Tab dialog box hasn't yet appeared, you should be in the Choose Database File dialog box. You can use this dialog box to locate the table query you want to use for your report. If you use a table, all the entries in the table are displayed in the report. If you use a query, only those entries that meet the requirements of the query are included in the report. (For more information about setting up a query, see Catalog⇨New Query.) If the table or query you select is not in the current catalog, you are asked to provide a description for the item before moving to the Cross-Tab dialog box.

Once you're in the Cross-Tab dialog box with the fields you need to use in the lower-right part of the screen (in the box labeled Fields), the rest is pretty straightforward. You use the entries in one of your groups to create the categories for the columns, and the entries in the other group for the rows. Simply drag one of the fields to the box for Rows and the other to the box for Columns. (Of course, you can also select the field and then use either the Add Row to Cross-Tab or Add Column to Cross-Tab buttons, but dragging is so much cooler.) To remove a field you put in the wrong spot, you can either drag it somewhere else or click it and use the Remove Field from Cross-Tab button.

The most important field, and the only one that's really required, is the one you want to summarize. In the flower example, that field is the number of bulbs. You drag the field containing the actual values to the Summarized Field box. If all you want is the totals for each combination of groups, you're done. Just click OK to see your report. The Cross-Tab dialog box shown here has the fields organized for the report shown previously.

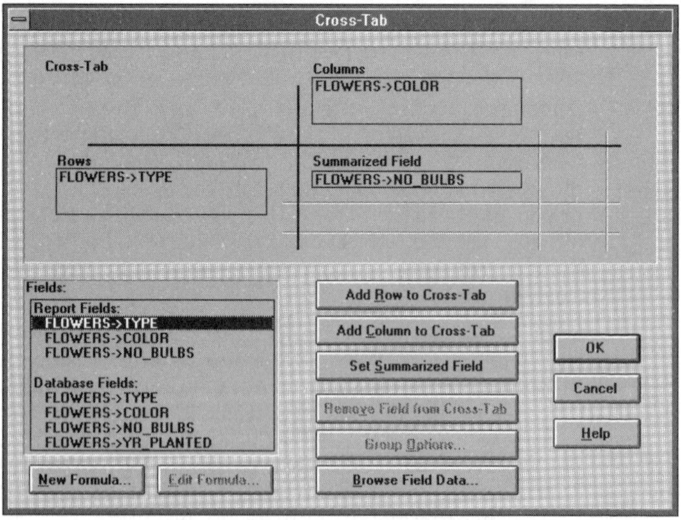

Unfortunately, your boss probably wants something a bit fancier, so, as usual, you have to do more work. The most likely thing you'll need to do is change how the groups are organized. It's easiest to do this before you view your report. If you are still in the Cross-Tab dialog box, click the group you want to work with and then select the Group Options button. If you've already viewed the report, click the heading for the group you want to change, click the right mouse button, and, from the menu that appears, select Change Cross-Tab Group Options. In the Cross-Tab Group Options dialog box, you can set in what order the categories are listed (generally, either ascending or descending) and what type of change should trigger a new category. The choices for what triggers a new category vary, depending upon what type of information is in the field.

In addition to formatting the various parts of your report (using the Format menu), you may also want to change how the information is summarized. The standard cross-tab totals the values for each category combination (for example, the total for red roses) as well as for both the row and column. To change the method used for the summary, you must be looking at your report and not at the Cross-Tab dialog box. To change the calculation for the entries, click the numeric format in the middle. To change the calculation for the rows, click the numeric format in the first row. To change the column, click the numeric format in the first column. Once you've selected the numeric format representing the summary to be changed, click the right mouse button. From the menu that appears, select Change Summary Operation. In the Summary Field dialog box, select the type of calculation you want and then click OK.

More stuff

To move from the Report view back to the Cross-Tab dialog box, move your cursor into the gray region on the left labeled Cross-Tab, click the right mouse button, and select Cross-Tab Layout.

In reality, you can use more than two fields for grouping your information. Both the Row and Column boxes can hold several field names. If you use more than one field, the entries in the second field are used as subcategories for the first field. For example, if you have entries for the shades of color (light, medium, and dark), you may use the color as the first field for the rows and shade as the second field. Your report would then be organized with a section for all the red flowers, and within that section would be lines for Light Red, Medium Red, and Dark Red.

Use the Browse Field Data button that appears on many of the dialog boxes to view a sampling of the contents of the currently selected field. This button can be very useful when you're trying to organize your report.

To learn how to add a calculated field to your report using the New Formula button, see Edit⇨Build Expression.

Catalog⇨New Form

Opens a new form and moves you into the Form Designer, where there are a variety of exciting tools for creating your own form. By the way, a form is primarily used to display information from your database *on-screen*, either for reviewing the information or for data entry. If you want to *print* the information, you should probably look at Catalog⇨New Report.

For keyboard krazies

For mouse maniacs

If you have the untitled form item selected, this button lets you create a new form.

Just the facts

Either select the untitled form item and then select Catalog⇨New Form, or just double-click on the untitled form. Actually, you have many options for getting to a new form, including Navigator⇨New Form and File⇨New⇨Form, but they all get you to the exact same place: the Form Expert dialog box. If you want to do things the tough way, select the Blank Form option and choose Create. When you create a blank form, you are taken immediately to the Form Designer, which is discussed under Catalog⇨Design Form.

If you want to do things the easy way (and if your form is fairly simple), select Expert Assistance and click the Next button. You then have to select a table or query to use on your form and once again click the Next button. If you are working with a catalog and the item you select is not in the catalog already, you are asked for a description. If asked, go ahead and humor your computer by providing one and then click OK. You now come to the most important screen in the entire Form Expert, the one where you decide which fields to include and their order. Although the specific field names will be different, the dialog box should look something like the one shown here.

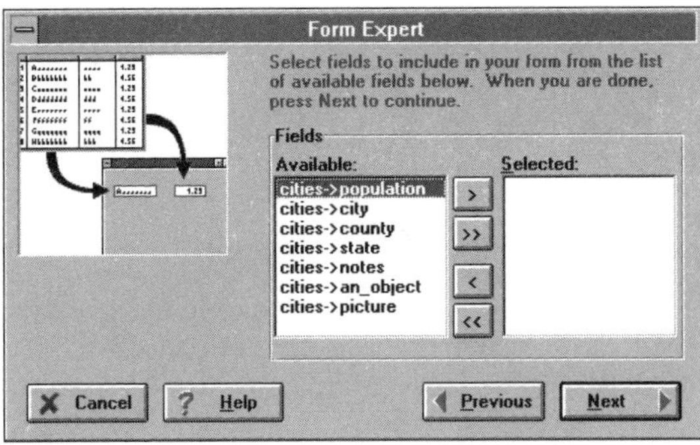

If you want all the fields in the same order as they appear in the table or query, just click the button with the double arrowhead pointing to the right (>>). If you want to move a single field, highlight the field and click the button with the single arrowhead pointing to the right (>). The buttons that point to the left are used to remove a field (<) or all the fields (<<) you've added by accident. After you've selected the fields you want on the form, click Next.

Your choices at this point should be among Columnar Layout, Form Layout, Browse Layout, and One to Many. Samples of the four layouts are shown in the upper left of the dialog box. For a description of the three most common layouts, see View⇨Columnar Layout, View⇨Form Layout, and View⇨Browse Layout. A one-to-many layout allows you to include another form on top of the first. This second form is called a *subform* and is used to display records from another table that are linked to the record displayed in the main form. Pick among the choices and click Next.

The final dialog box in the Form Expert lets you format the various items on the form. You can select the text and colors for the title, any text you add to the form (such as labels for the fields), and the actual entries in each field. The example in the upper-left corner of the dialog box changes to show you the results of the options you have selected. When you're finished, click Create. (You thought I was going to say Next, didn't you?)

This drops you into the Form Designer with the form that the Form Expert has created for you. Now, the tough stuff. If you aren't happy with what you have, you need to make changes to the form by hand (and if you started with a blank form, I'll assume you're not satisfied with it). The use of the various tools for designing a form are discussed under Catalog⇨Design Form.

More stuff

To change the source for the fields in your form, select any control with a DataLink property. In the Properties window, select the DataLink property and click the wrench button at the right of the box. In the Choose Field dialog box, click the View button and then use the resulting dialog box to select the source for the fields.

To find out more than you want to know about creating your own forms with the Form Expert, see Chapter 10 in *dBASE For Windows For Dummies*.

You can work with a form by using Catalog⇨Run Form or any of its equivalents.

Catalog⇨New Labels

Creates a new set of labels using Crystal Reports. This process has two steps: formatting the page for the labels and then placing and formatting the fields on a sample label.

For keyboard krazies

For mouse maniacs

With the untitled labels item selected, this button opens Crystal Reports with a new, blank set of labels.

Just the facts

Unless you've already been using Crystal Reports with one of the open databases, the very first thing you see when you create a new set of labels is the Open Table Required dialog box, where you can select a table or query to use as the source for the fields on your labels. After selecting the source and clicking OK, you find yourself in the Mailing Labels dialog box shown in this figure. If dBASE assumes you want to use the same table as you did before, then you won't have to deal with the Open Table Required dialog box and will jump right to this screen.

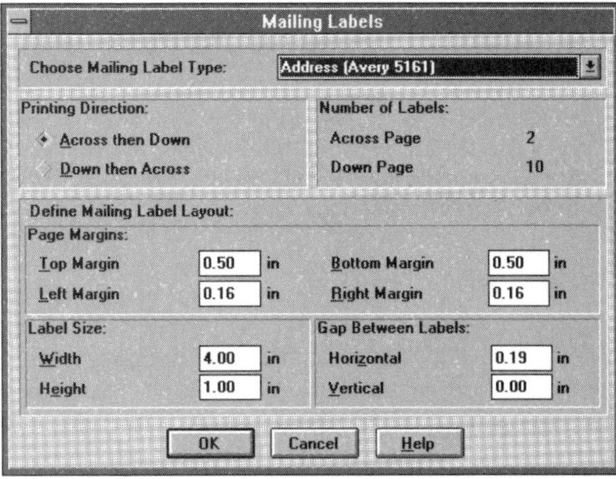

Select a predefined set of labels from the list at the top of the box, or use the boxes in the bottom half to define the margins on the page and the size of the individual labels. The number of labels on the page is then calculated using the values you provide. Whenever possible, use a predefined style of labels — it's easier and gives much more predictable results. If you need to change the size of the page, define the margins and label size and then click OK. Once you've created your untitled sheet of labels, you can use File⇨Printer Setup to change the description of the physical page.

After you define the arrangement of labels on the page, you can then drag the fields you want into position from the Insert Database Field dialog box. Use the commands on the Format menu within Crystal Reports to control the look of the text on your labels and for greater control over position. The dotted lines on the label sheet mark the recommended borders of the label. Although you can place fields so that they extend beyond these borders, you risk cutting off the contents if the entry is too long.

More stuff

If you're going to create a label for every record in your table, base your labels on the table. Use a query if you want to pick and choose which records are included when you print the labels.

For more on setting up mailing labels, see Chapter 21 in *dBASE For Windows For Dummies*.

Catalog⇨New Query

Opens the Query Designer, where you can create a new query using any of the available tables. Queries form the basis for most of your database tasks, including locating records within the database and selecting records for reports.

For keyboard krazies

For mouse maniacs

With the untitled query item selected, this button creates a new query.

Just the facts

The first thing you need to do is select the primary database table for your query. Generally, this is the table that contains most of the fields that you want in your results. If the Open Table Required dialog box appears, you can use it to select one of the database tables; otherwise, you can add tables from within the Query Designer by using Query⇨Add Table. Each table in the query is displayed separately as a *Table Entry* with the field names in the top row and blanks for adding the query conditions below each field name. (See the figure somewhere near here.) If the fields in the table don't all fit on a single screen, you can use the left- and right-arrow buttons at the left of the table entry to change which fields are displayed.

If you want to remove a table, select it by clicking it once and then select Query⇨Remove Selected Table. Many queries only use one table, but sometimes the answer to your question requires combining information from several different tables. In that case, you need to define the relationships among the tables using Query⇨Set Relation. The figure here shows three tables and the relations among them.

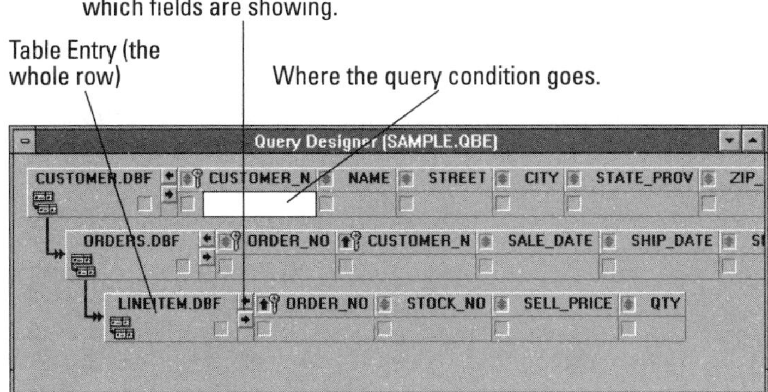

The relations among tables are shown by the lines on the left and the up-arrows in the linking cells (ORDER_NO and CUSTOMER_N). The key symbol indicates that all the fields are also indexed, which means the query should be processed a bit faster.

The next step is to decide which fields you want to see in the results. To display a field in the results, click the small box below the field name. A green check mark signifies that the field will be indicated in the results. To include all the fields from a table, click the small box at the left end of the table entry. Notice from the example that you can include any combination of fields from the linked table. In general, you only include one or the other of the linked fields. In other words, check only one of the CUSTOMER_N fields; otherwise, each record in the query results will show the value for that field twice.

Finally, you are ready to define the *conditions* for your query. The conditions are the rules for selecting which records are included in the query results. Only those records that match all the listed conditions are displayed in the query results. If you want to see all the records in the tables, don't include any conditions. In most cases, however, the whole point of using a query is to limit what is displayed.

A condition for a query consists of an *operator* followed by a value. An operator tells dBASE how to compare the value to the entry in the field for each record. Different types of values require special symbols. For example, if you want to use some text as your value, you need to enclose it in quotation marks (either "Bob" or 'Bob'). If you want to use a date, you need to enclose it in curly brackets ({ and }). Because numbers are used so often in queries, they don't require any special symbols.

The simplest format for a condition is just entering a value in one of the fields. One way to do this is to enter an equal sign (=) followed by the value, instructing dBASE to include only the records that have *this* value in *this* field. You can also use the pound sign (#) followed by a value to include only records *without* this value in this field. A related operator is the dollar sign ($), which causes dBASE to include all records in which this field contains this value — even if the field also contains other things.

When you are working with fields that contain numbers, you often want to see all the records above or below a certain value. To do that, you can use the greater than (>), less than (<), greater than or equal to (<=), and less than or equal to (>=) operators. In the example shown in this figure, the query will list all customers who are named "Bob" and who have ordered more than five items.

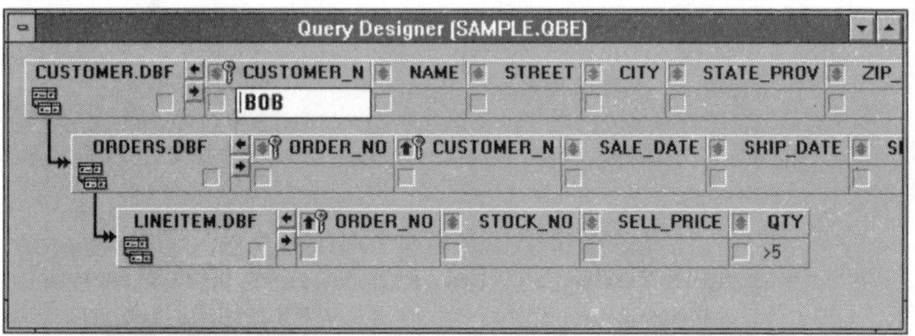

You can combine as many conditions into a single query as you wish. Usually, the more conditions, the fewer records that will match. If you want to include more than one condition for a single field, you need to decide whether the match must meet all the conditions or just any one of the conditions. If a record must meet all the conditions, separate the conditions for the field with commas (,). For example, for a condition to list only records where the value in the field is greater than 500 and less than 1000 (in other words, between 500 and 1000), you would enter **>500, <1000** as the condition. If a record need only match any one of the conditions, each condition goes on a separate line under the field name. To get a new line, press the down-arrow on your keyboard.

You have two special sets of symbols at your disposal when trying to match dates. Two curly brackets with nothing between them match any records that do not contain a date in that field. Two angle brackets (<>) match any records with a valid date.

To see those records that match your conditions, select View⇨Query Results.

More stuff

The results of a query are displayed in a table format, which can be very hard to read. For more readable results, you should create a form or report and base it on the query. Save your query under a filename that you can recognize later. Then, instead of selecting a table for your form or report, select the query.

For the basics of setting up a query, see Chapter 12 in *dBASE For Windows For Dummies*. Designing your conditions for your queries can be a very complex topic. For more information, see Chapter 13 in *dBASE For Windows For Dummies*.

Catalog⇨New Report

Opens Crystal Reports with a new, blank report screen. You must base your report either on a database table or on a query. Fortunately, you can change what your report is based on after creating the blank report as long as the field types are the same in both the old and new table or query.

For keyboard krazies

For mouse maniacs

If you've selected the untitled report item, this button opens Crystal Reports with a blank report.

Just the facts

The first thing you need to understand about a report is that it can only contain entries for those fields that are in the table or query you are using as the basis for the report. If you want to combine information from several tables, you must first create a query that uses all those tables. Once you associate your report with a table or query (using either the Open Table Required dialog box or the Database⇨File Location command), you are ready to add text and fields to your report.

Before you begin adding things, however, you need to understand the fundamental formatting feature of reports: *sections*. A section is a portion of a report that is formatted differently from other parts and is defined either by its position on the page or by the type of information it contains. For example, three sections appear on your blank report: Page Header, Page Footer, and

Details. The Page Header and Page Footer sections are based on position and appear at the top and bottom of each page (just like your head and feet appear at the top and bottom of your body). The Details section is defined by its contents: It prints the details for each and every record in the report.

The first thing you need to decide is what sections you want to add. Note that you can add only content-based sections, not those based on position. Add sections whenever you want to summarize values for a group or insert a new heading at the start of a group. For example, if you have information about the populations of all the cities in the U.S., you may want to group the information first by state and then by individual counties. To add a new section, use Insert⇨Group Section. When you add a new section, you get both a group header above the Details section and a group footer below the Details section. Add your sections starting with the most general. That way the most general appears first and the more specific appear within the general sections. The figure shown here is organized so that the cities (in the Details section) are grouped by county within the state. The values used to define a group must be sorted in your report.

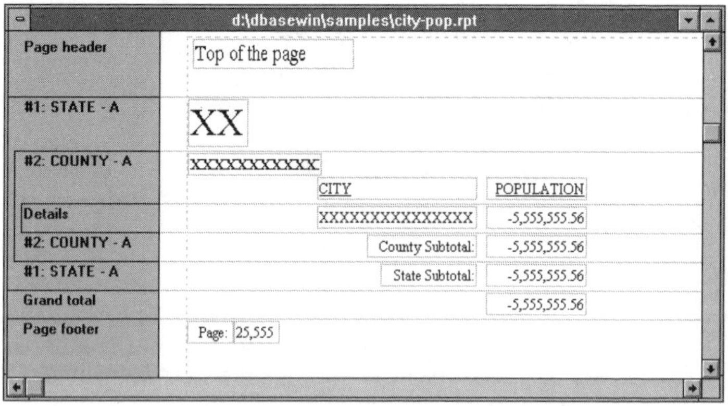

Once you've figured out which sections you need, you should decide what you want to put into each section. Generally, headers include text, field names, and the field used to define the section; footers contain formula fields, which let you summarize the values for a field for all the records included in the section. To create a formula field, use Insert⇨Formula Field. To add a field to your report, use Insert⇨Database Field. To add text, click on the report and start typing, or use Insert⇨Text Field. (All of these are Crystal Reports commands and not covered in this quick reference.) If you need to change the size of a section, position your cursor over the bottom edge of the section and, after the cursor changes to a line with arrowheads on either side, drag the edge to its new location.

Once you've added all the fields to your report, use the commands on the Crystal Reports Insert menu to add lines, boxes, and graphics to more clearly mark the boundaries of your sections. You can also add special fields such as the page number or current date by using Insert⇨Special Field. The Crystal Reports Format menu can then be used to make the contents of your report more attractive. Use the Format⇨Section command to control things such as page breaks and how the section is organized.

More stuff

For an example of creating a simple report, see Chapter 17 in *dBASE For Windows For Dummies*. For a more sophisticated report, see Chapter 19 in *dBASE For Windows For Dummies*.

Catalog⇨New Table

Creates a new table, which is where the actual information in your database is stored. Creating a table is the first step in creating your own database system.

For keyboard krazies

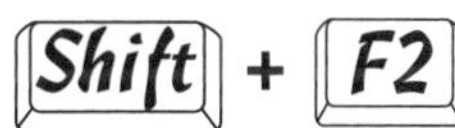

For mouse maniacs

With the untitled table items selected, this button creates a new table.

Just the facts

Before you start working at the keyboard, you need to design the structure of your table. The most important question is, What fields will be included? (A field is a category of information — first name or street address, for example.) You want to make sure that you include a field for any information you may need later, but you also want to use as few fields as possible. This leads to such exciting discussions as whether you should use one field for a person's name or three fields — one for first name, one for middle name, and one for last name. It really depends on what you are going to use the database for. If you plan to have a full-name field *and* a Dear-first-name field for a letter, for example, then I recommend three discrete fields.

Once you've decided which fields to include, you need to decide what type of information should go into each field (the field *type*) and how big the fields should be (field size). The most common choices for type are character, memo, numeric, date, and logical. A character field can contain anything but is limited in size; for large amounts of text, use a memo field. Numeric fields contain things that you intend to use for math — not necessarily everything that contains numbers, but rather just those things that you may use for calculations. For example, even though phone numbers contain numbers, they're always stored in a character field. Otherwise, dBASE would take the phone number 555-1212 and try to subtract 1212 from 555. With numeric fields, you tell dBASE how many digits to display after the decimal by placing a value in the Decimal box. Date fields contain dates. No surprise there. They have to be eight characters wide — two for month, a slash, two for day, a slash, and two for year. Finally, logical fields can contain only one of two choices: true or false (also known as Yes and No).

Once you've gathered all this information, you are ready to actually enter the information into the computer. Select Catalog⇨New Table and you'll get a screen like the one shown here.

Table Structure (CITIES.DBF)

Name: CITIES.DBF Type: DBASE

Updated: 11/01/94 Bytes Used: 70

Records: 17 Bytes Left: 32,697

Field	Name	Type	Width	Decimal	Index
1		Numeric	10	0	Ascend
2	CITY	Character	15	0	Ascend
3	COUNTY	Character	12	0	None
4	STATE	Character	2	0	None
5	NOTES	Memo	10	0	None
6	AN_OBJECT	OLE	10	0	None
7	PICTURE	Binary	10	0	None

Each field has to have a name composed of all uppercase letters and no spaces. You should try to select names that you'll recognize later and that have some meaning. Unfortunately, dBASE's restrictions make it hard to use truly meaningful names. Enter the name and Tab over to the Type list. Select the type for the field and then use Tab to move to any other boxes that must be completed for the field. The final choice, Index, lets you define an index for the field. An index makes searching for a match within the field faster, but the more indexes you have, the slower dBASE works with the table. You should only index those fields that you intend to search often.

After you've filled in all the necessary information, press Tab again to get a new line for defining another field. When you've added all the fields you need, select View⇨Table Records to begin entering the actual information.

More stuff

While designing your table, you'll often discover that you need more than one table. If you have a field that is going to contain the same information throughout many of your records, you may want to put that field into a separate table and link it to your first table using a special field for that purpose. For example, suppose you're creating a database to track your customers' orders. Rather than repeat a customer's address each time an order is sent in, you may create a table with the customer information and assign each customer a unique customer code. Then, in your orders table, you can use just that code (rather than all the customer's information) to identify the order.

There are two other types of fields that you may want to use — Binary and OLE. Binary fields can hold pictures or sounds, and OLE fields can hold anything created by a Windows program. Each of these fields uses its own commands and special tools (specifically the OLE Viewer, Sound Player, and Image Viewer). For more information, try checking the index for references to these field types or the tools used to work with them.

For the basics of designing your own table, see Chapter 4 in *dBASE For Windows For Dummies*. To find out about editing your data, see Chapter 5 in *dBASE For Windows For Dummies*. To find out how to change the table structure, or about special formatting for fields, see Chapter 8 in *dBASE For Windows For Dummies*.

Use the commands on the Structure menu to add or delete fields. You can always change which fields are indexed within a table by using Table⇨Table Utilities⇨Manage Indexes or one of its equivalents. You can control how the contents of each field are displayed and what type of information can be put into each field by using Properties⇨Table Records Window.

Catalog⇨Run Form

Opens the selected form for your use. If the form is based on a query, only those records that match the query are displayed.

For keyboard krazies

For mouse maniacs

This button uses the selected query to create a table of records.

Just the facts

Select the form you want to use and then choose Catalog⇨Run Form. Of course, you can also just double-click on the form.

More stuff

If you want to make changes to the form, you need to use Catalog⇨Design Form.

Catalog⇨Run Labels

Opens the selected labels so that you can preview them on-screen and then print them. Working with labels this way does not require that you open Crystal Reports.

For keyboard krazies

For mouse maniacs

This button opens the selected labels so you can preview them or print them.

Just the facts

Select the label file. Select Catalog⇨Run Labels. 'Nuff said.

More stuff

You can just double-click a label item to open it.

To make changes to the labels, open Crystal Reports and load the label definitions by selecting the labels and then selecting Catalog⇨Design Labels. Use the commands on the Label menu to move between labels; use the commands on the View menu to control how the labels are displayed.

Catalog⇨Run Query

Activates the stored query and displays the results. To *change* the conditions used in the query, see Catalog⇨Design Query.

For keyboard krazies

For mouse maniacs

This button lets you view the results of a stored query.

Just the facts

If you just want to see the results of the query using the stored conditions, select the query and then select Catalog⇨Run Query. If you want to make changes to the query after viewing the results, use View⇨Query Design.

Catalog⇨Run Report

Previews the selected report on the screen and lets you print the report without having to open Crystal Reports.

For keyboard krazies

For mouse maniacs

This button opens the selected report and displays it on-screen so that you can preview or print it.

Just the facts

Select the report and then select Catalog➪Run Report. I don't think it could be much simpler.

More stuff

If the report is based on a query and you want to change which records are included in the report, select the query and use Catalog➪Design Query.

Edit➪Build Expression

Opens the Expression Builder, which is a tool for helping you build expressions. Of course, it would be rather weird if the Expression Builder enabled you to build origami swans. An expression, in case you're interested, is a formula or set of instructions used to calculate a value or select records.

For keyboard krazies

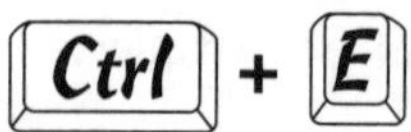

For mouse maniacs

This button only appears when you are editing a program.

This button appears at the end of text boxes where you can open a builder to get help. It often opens the Expression Builder.

Just the facts

When it's available, the Expression Builder is a very useful tool. You're more likely to encounter it when you click the wrench icon while working with a property value or while creating rules for selecting records in a report. The empty Expression Builder window is shown here.

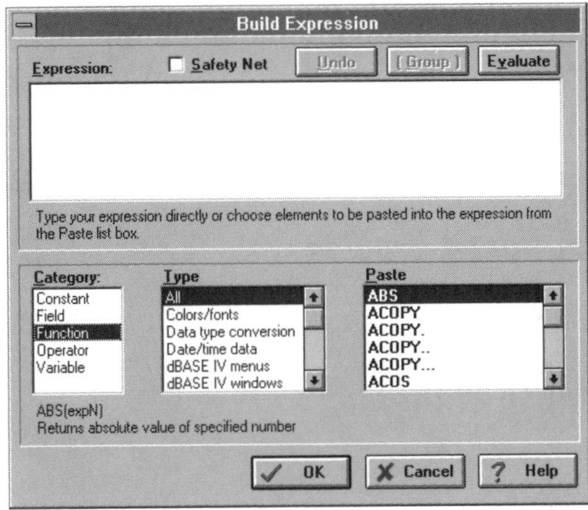

Use the lists at the bottom of the screen to select items to be pasted into your formula. Other parts of the formula, including the symbols for performing calculations, can be entered from the keyboard. Unfortunately, it's generally just as easy to type in your formula the long way as to use the Expression Builder. Nice idea, lousy design.

Edit⇨Convert Case

Changes the text so that the letters are uppercase, lowercase, or just having the first letter of each word in uppercase (often called *initial caps*).

Just the facts

The most difficult thing about using this command is finding a time when it is available. You'll find it if you're working with a memo field and want to change which letters are capitalized; you can highlight the text and then select Edit⇨Convert Case. You aren't done yet because there's a submenu off to the right where you have to pick which of the three styles you want to use (Uppercase, Lowercase, or Initial Capitals). To get to the text stored in a memo field, double-click the page icon showing in the field.

Edit➪Copy

Takes whatever is selected, puts it on the internal Xerox machine, and puts the copy onto your Clipboard. This is useful when you want to place the same information in more than one location.

For keyboard krazies

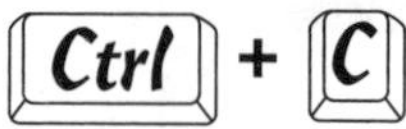

For mouse maniacs

This button copies whatever you select onto your Clipboard.

Just the facts

There are basically four steps (and two commands) involved in using Edit➪Copy. The first step is to highlight the information you want to make a copy of. Next, select Edit➪Copy. This action puts a copy of whatever you had highlighted onto the Clipboard. You then need to move to where you want the new copy of the information. You can use any of the methods that you know for moving, none of which will change what's on the Clipboard. To actually insert the information from the Clipboard, select Edit➪Paste. That's all there is to it. If you want to put the information in more than one spot, simply move to another location and select Edit➪Paste again. You can paste as many times as you want to make your copies. Note that only one thing can be on the Clipboard at a time. If you copy (or cut) something new, the old information is thrown out.

More stuff

When you are working with a report or mailing labels, you can use the command to copy items from one section to another or to copy text within an item.

You can use the Copy command to copy the information from several fields into a new record, or you can copy an entire record. If you want to make a new record, you need to use Edit➪Paste Add Records rather than the plain old Edit➪Paste.

If you want to replace some old information with what you have just copied, highlight the old information before selecting Edit➪Paste.

If you want to move information, you first use Edit➪Cut. Then, to get the information off of the Clipboard to where you want it moved, you need to use Edit➪Paste.

Edit⇨Copy to File

Makes a file containing a copy of whatever you had selected. The original is left unchanged. You can use this to create a file containing part or all of the information in a memo field.

Just the facts

Select the text that you want to store in a separate file and then select Edit⇨Copy to File. You are presented with a Save As dialog box where you can enter the name of the file. Generally, dBASE does put a TXT extension at the end of the filename for you. If you want a different extension, you have to add it yourself. The exception is when you are working with part of a dBASE program, in which case dBASE suggests the extension PRG.

More stuff

If you want to make a file that contains a copy of a report, use File⇨Print⇨File within Crystal Reports. If you want a file containing records from a database, use Table⇨Table Utilities⇨Export Records.

Edit⇨Cut

Takes the selected information out of the database and puts it onto the Clipboard. This is the first step in moving something.

For keyboard krazies

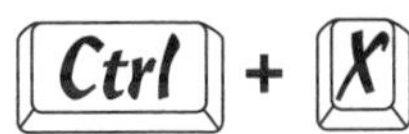

For mouse maniacs

This button cuts selected data from your database and puts it onto the Clipboard.

Just the facts

There are basically four steps (and two commands) involved in using Edit⇨Cut. The first step is to let dBASE know what information you want to work with by highlighting what you want to move. Next, select Edit⇨Cut. What you had highlighted disappears and is stored on the Clipboard. You then need to move to where you want to put the information. You can use any of the methods that you know for moving, as none of them will change what's on the Clipboard. To actually insert the information, select Edit⇨Paste. That's all there is to it. The information is gone from its old position and inserted where you now want it. Remember that only one thing can be on the Clipboard at a time. If you copy (or cut) something new, the old information on the Clipboard is thrown out.

Just as with Edit⇨Copy, you can put the information in more than one spot. Simply move to another location and select Edit⇨Paste again. You can paste as many times as you want to make your new copies. Also, if you want to replace some old information with what you have just copied, highlight the old information before selecting Edit⇨Paste.

More stuff

You can use the Cut command to move information from one record to another. If you want to make a new record with the information, you need to use Edit⇨Paste Add Records rather the plain old Edit⇨Paste. You may use this method if, for example, two of your friends get divorced and you need to make a new record for each of them in your address book (rather than having them on a single record).

If you want to get rid of something without disturbing the contents of the Clipboard, use Edit⇨Delete (or Edit⇨Clear if you're working in Crystal Reports). You need to use Edit⇨Paste to insert information from the Clipboard into your database.

Edit⇨Delete

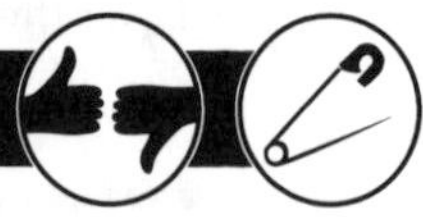

Removes the information. It's gone. The only way to bring it back is to use Edit⇨Undo.

For keyboard krazies

For mouse maniacs

Use this button to delete information.

Just the facts

This command is (unfortunately) one of the easiest commands to use. Just highlight what you want to get rid of and press the Delete key (Del). It's a real bummer to have something highlighted, reach for another key, and hit Delete by mistake. If that happens to you, use Edit⇨Undo right away.

More stuff

This command can be deadly if you are using the Navigator. If you have an item selected and press the Delete key (or select Edit⇨Delete), you are starting to remove the file from that item from your disk. If you remove the file from your disk, there's no easy method for getting it back. Fortunately, you do get a dialog box asking whether you really mean to do this. Be sure to stop and think about it before clicking Yes. By the way, the same actions in a catalog aren't as dangerous because you are only removing the item from the catalog, not from the disk.

If you want a copy of the information placed on the Clipboard, use Edit⇨Cut. Putting the information onto the Clipboard rather than deleting it enables you to move it to a new location.

Edit⇨Insert from File

Takes the entire contents of a file and sticks it into your database at the insertion point. This is particularly useful for inserting large blocks of text into memo fields. You also use this command to insert pictures or sounds into a binary field.

Just the facts

To add a text file, you need to first open the text editor for the memo field by double-clicking on the page icon that appears within the field. To add a picture or sound, you need to double-click on the binary field and then choose between adding a picture (with Image Viewer) or sound (with Sound Player). You can also open a field by selecting View⇨Field Contents.

You can then select Edit⇨Insert from File to open a dialog box where you can select the file to insert. Once you've located the file, double-click on the filename to insert the file's contents into the field.

More stuff

To save something from a memo field in a file, use Edit⇨Copy to File.

Edit⇨Insert Object

Puts an "object" created with another program into your database. An object can be pretty much anything such as a recording of sound, a picture, or even a movie.

Just the facts

If you create a field of the OLE type, you can double-click on the field's contents to work with the OLE Viewer. A common example (though in reality somewhat unrealistic) is that every record in the personnel file contains a sample of the individual's voice. Each voice is different, so the object is in a field rather than on the background. Using OLE offers tremendous advantages for sophisticated databases, but they are more than what normal folk ever need worry about.

However, since you paid your money, I'll give you a quick overview of inserting objects. First, open an OLE field (by double-clicking on it). Then, go to where you want the object and select Edit⇨Insert Object. You get the following dialog box:

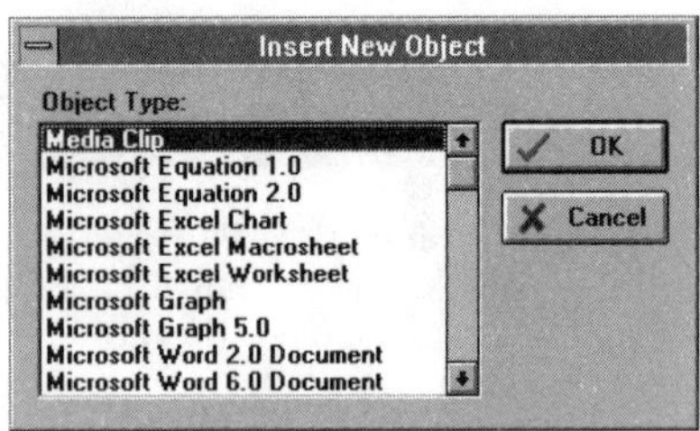

Talk about your strange dialog boxes. The content of this one changes based on what you have installed on your computer, but the process is fairly straight forward once you decide what type of object you want. To create a new object that will just exist within your database, you need to pick the type of object you want in the Object Type list. Highlight the object type (based on the program that will create it, such as an Excel Spreadsheet) and click on OK (or press Enter). You're now in the other program where you will create the object. Do whatever you need to create the object (after buying the appropriate *...For Dummies* book and its accompanying *Dummies Quick Reference*) and then select the last command on the File menu. It's probably something like Exit and Return to dBASE. That's it. The object has been inserted.

More stuff

The Object Type list can include programs that you once had but are now deleted (or at least temporarily taken off of your system). The problem is that the available objects are registered when a program is added, and there isn't a standard way to remove them. Just restrict your choices to the programs you know on your machine.

You need to use the Edit⇨Object command to make changes to the object. You use Edit⇨Links to manage any files used to hold the objects.

Edit⇨Join Text Lines

Gets rid of the paragraph marks at the ends of text and sticks the lines together. This is useful when you need to reformat a bunch of text that was originally created as separate lines, but which you now want formatted with word-wrap.

Just the facts

Select the lines you want to join and select Edit⇨Join Text Lines. You need to make sure that you've selected the end of one line and the start of the next if you want them to be joined together. dBASE puts the second line after the first and inserts a space between the last character on the first line and the first character on the second.

Edit⇨Links

Controls the links between objects in your database and the files that contain those objects. This allows you to reference an object that is stored in a separate file from your report or in your database. With a link, the copy in your dBASE file can be updated if there are changes made to the source.

Just the facts

Changing where dBASE looks for the files used by an OLE link is very easy. All you have to do is select the Edit⇨Links command in dBASE and you're shown a dialog box like this one listing all of the existing links. You need to select the link you wish to work with by clicking on it.

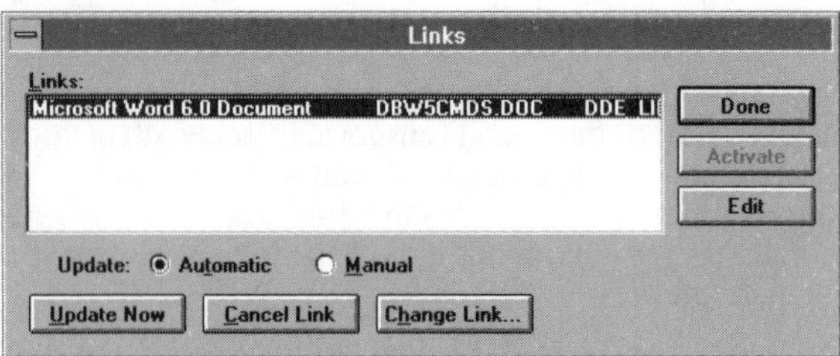

One of the more common things you may need to do with a link is to change the source for the link. Changing the source, of course, usually changes what is actually inserted. To change which file dBASE is using for the information, select Change Source. You get a dialog box that you can use to move around on your hard disk until you find the new file that you want to use.

You can also use the appropriate dialog box to break a link by using the Cancel Link button (in dBASE). When you break an OLE link, the information is permanently inserted into your document and cannot be edited by the original program.

You can elect to have the link updated automatically by selecting Automatic in dBASE. If you'd rather, you can set the link so that the system only checks for changes in the source when you request it. To do that, simply set the link as Manual. Then to update the information, select the link and click on the Update Now button. The information that is currently in the linked file will be used to update the field.

More stuff

When a field is displaying information contained in a linked file, accidentally deleting the file will not cause the image to change. You will, however, run into problems if you try to update that link manually. Because the file no longer exists, your system won't be able to find any information, and the object will be deleted. If you intend to delete the link to a file, you should break the link first so that a copy of the information remains in your dBASE file.

If you have a group of files that are used as objects in your database, you may want to create a special subdirectory for them. That way, if you need to move the database to another system, you can copy all of the linked files easily. When first creating the link, move the file to the subdirectory first. Otherwise, you'll have to use Edit⇨Links to change the link after you move the file.

If you want to edit a linked object, simply double-click on the object (or select the object and use Edit⇨Object). The program that created the object will open (assuming it is available). In dBASE, you can select the link in the Edit Link dialog box and click on the Edit button.

Before you use Edit⇨Links, you must have already created a link using Edit⇨Paste Link.

Edit⇨Object

Opens the program used to create the selected object. An "object" is anything that was created by a separate program and that is still managed by that program. For example, if you have a database of film clips, the film clips are inserted as objects into your database but managed by another program. Any changes need to be made by using that other program. One of things to watch out for is that the name of this command changes slightly depending upon the type of object selected. It always contains the word *object*, but sometimes you get more of a description (such as Edit⇨Paintbrush Object.)

For mouse maniacs

This button activates the object. Sometimes this is very important. For example, it plays a sound object. For many objects, there is no difference between the effects of two buttons.

This button opens the selected OLE object and the program that created it so that you can make changes to the object.

Just the facts

You just need to select the object that you want to edit and select Edit⇨Object. Be warned that the name of the command changes to reflect the type of object that you're going to be working with (Excel Spreadsheet Object or Paintbrush Picture Object). Very often, you will find that there is a submenu with choices such as Play, Open, or Edit. At other times, the only choice will be selecting the Edit⇨Object command itself. The Play option appears for objects such as sound recordings, movie clips, or animation and causes the object to activate (play the sound or show the movie). The Open or Edit options (or if the Object command is the only option) open the program that created the object so that you can make changes. At that point, you need to find the ...*For Dummies* book for whichever product created the object.

More stuff

For most images, double-clicking will open the program that created the object and allow you to make changes. When an object has a Play option, you'll need to use the menu in order to edit the object — double-clicking will just activate the object (such as playing sound or showing animation).

See Edit⇨Links for information about changing where dBASE looks for the linked file and Edit⇨Insert Object or Edit⇨Paste Link for information about adding an OLE object.

Edit⇨Paste

Takes whatever is on the Clipboard and inserts it into your database. How does an object get onto the Clipboard? Good question. You use either Edit⇨Cut or Edit⇨Copy to put it there.

For keyboard krazies

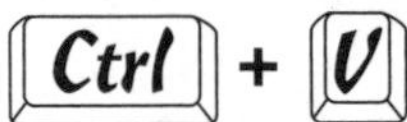

For mouse maniacs

Inserts whatever happens to be on the Clipboard (which got there because you used either Edit⇨Copy or Edit⇨Cut).

Just the facts

In order for this command to do any good, you must have put something onto the Clipboard by using either Edit⇨Copy or Edit⇨Cut. The Edit⇨Paste command takes the contents of the Clipboard and inserts them at the cursor. The only restriction is that if you are pasting into a field, dBASE must be able to convert the information to the proper format for the field type. You can paste the same thing into different locations as many times as you want.

More stuff

The information that you are pasting can be part of the contents of a field, one or more entire fields, an entire record, a control, or even information from another program. The only requirement is that the location be of the right type to hold the pasted information. In other words, you can't paste a picture into a field designed to hold text.

If you have anything selected, Edit⇨Paste will replace that information with whatever is in the Clipboard.

If you're working with a table (the standard view of a table or the results of a query), the information is pasted based upon shape. If there is information that won't fit (for example, you're on the last row and the Clipboard contains two rows' worth of information), the "extra" information will just be dropped. It's still on the Clipboard, but it won't be added to your document. To add the records, you need to use Edit⇨Paste Add Records. If you are working with a form and have information on the Clipboard that was contained in fields that don't exist on the form, the information for those fields will be dropped (though they're still on the Clipboard).

To learn all about putting things onto the Clipboard, see Edit⇨Cut (for moving things) or Edit⇨Copy.

Edit⇨Paste Add Records

Creates new records using the information on the Clipboard. Of course, you need to have put proper information on the Clipboard by using the Edit⇨Cut or Edit⇨Copy commands.

Just the facts

It doesn't matter where you are in the database table when you select Edit⇨Paste Add Records because the new records are always added at the end of the table.

More stuff

You are most likely to use this command to duplicate existing records that already have most of the information you need in your new record. Start by selecting an entire record (or more than one adjacent record by dragging across the record numbers). Then select Edit⇨Copy and then Edit⇨Paste Add Records. Copies of the selected records are added at the end of the table. You can then make whatever changes are necessary to the new records.

Edit⇨Paste Link

Creates a link between information from another program and an OLE field within dBASE. You have to copy the information in the other program and then move to dBASE to paste the link.

Just the facts

The first step is to put the information (whether it's a picture, sounds, or whatever) onto the Clipboard. You do this by using Edit⇨Copy in the program where you created the stuff. (You can use Edit⇨Cut, but it's generally better to leave the original and use Copy instead.) If dBASE is already opened, you can switch to it by holding down the Alt key and continually pressing Tab until the name dBASE 5.0 for Windows appears in the box in the center of your screen. If dBASE isn't opened, you need to open it from the Program Manager.

Once you're in dBASE, you need to move the OLE field that is to contain the information and open the OLE Viewer (by double-clicking on the field). Then, and only then, can you select Edit⇨Paste Link. A copy of the information is now displayed in the OLE Viewer.

More stuff

I can consistently crash my entire system by selecting something within dBASE, selecting Edit⇨Copy, opening an OLE field, and trying to use Edit⇨Paste Link. This is not a feature — it's a bug, a bad thing, evil, and not nice.

To manage your links, use Edit⇨Links. For more on inserting objects (rather than linking to them), see Edit⇨Insert Object.

Edit⇨Search⇨Bottom Line

Really, this should be something involving the words *go to* because all it does is move you to the last line in a memo field or in a program file.

For keyboard krazies

Just the facts

Select Edit⇨Search⇨Bottom Line and, faster than you can count, you are moved to the end of whatever you are working with. This is particularly useful when working in memo fields so that you can add more information at the end of what's already there.

More stuff

To move to the start of the memo field or program, use Edit⇨Search⇨Top Line.

Edit⇨Search⇨Find Next Text

Repeats the current search within a memo field or program. This lets you move from one matching bit of text to another without having to open the Find Text dialog box.

For keyboard krazies

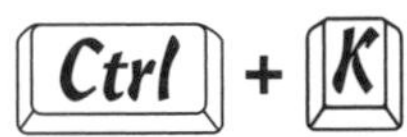

Just the facts

In order to use Edit⇨Search⇨Find Next Text, you need to have already searched for some text using Edit⇨Search⇨Find Text. As soon as you select Edit⇨Search⇨Find Next Text (or press Ctrl+K), dBASE moves to the next match within the current memo field or program. To use the command, you must have first opened the memo field or program file.

More stuff

To start searching for matching text in a memo field or program, use Edit⇨Search⇨Find Text. To look for matches in any of the fields within your database table, use Table⇨Find Records.

Edit⇨Search⇨Find Text

Finds the text you are looking for in the current memo field or within a program. If you want to look for something in the fields of your table, you need to use Table⇨Find Records.

For keyboard krazies

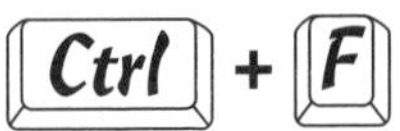

For mouse maniacs

Opens the Find Text dialog box so that you can search for text within a memo field or program.

Just the facts

First things first — enter the text that you want to look for in the Find What box. dBASE tries to help you out by inserting the text that you were working with (either the selection or the word containing the insertion cursor), but it's easy enough to change. Just start typing, and the new text replaces whatever was in the box. If you select Find, dBASE moves to where the characters you typed can be found.

Of course, you can have more control over exactly how dBASE searches for and matches your text. First, you can choose between having dBASE search Up (towards the start of the document) or Down (towards the end of the document).

You can also choose between having dBASE match the characters wherever they occur or only when they appear as a separate phrase (set off by spaces, punctuation, or some combination). To find the characters wherever they appear, make sure the Match Whole Words option is cleared. If the Match Case box is cleared, dBASE treats capital letters (uppercase) and lowercase letters interchangeably. That means that dBASE, dbase, and DBASE would all match each other. With the Match Case box checked, only characters that exactly match what is in the Find What box are found.

More stuff

To repeat your search, use Edit⇨Search⇨Find Next Text. To look for records that contain text, use Table⇨Find Records.

Edit⇨Search⇨Go to Line Number

In a memo field or program, moves you to the requested line number. The first line is number 1, and each additional line (whether it contains text or not) counts as another line.

For keyboard krazies

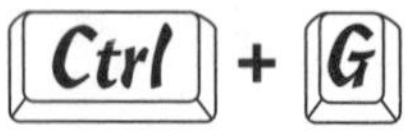

Just the facts

Not too surprisingly, there is a dialog box in which you can enter the line number. Just select Edit⇨Search⇨Go to Line Number, type the line number you want, and press Enter. Suddenly, faster than Dorothy in the *Wizard of Oz*, you're in Kansas. OK, I'm kidding. You just get moved to the line you asked for. Actually, that's fine because you probably didn't want to go to Kansas anyway. Not that I have anything against Kansas, but I'd probably rather go to New York or Hawaii.

More stuff

To find something in a memo field or program, use Edit⇨Search⇨Find Text.

Edit⇨Search⇨Replace Text

Gives you an easy way to find everywhere that you wrote *Lotus 1–2–3* and replace it with *Novell Quattro Pro*. This can come in very handy if you write computer books. The only problem is that it only works in memo fields or within programs.

For keyboard krazies

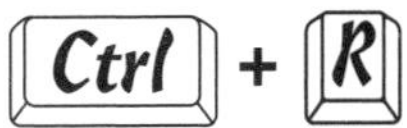

For mouse maniacs

Opens a dialog box where you can enter text to search for as well as what you want to use to replace the text with once you find it.

Just the facts

To start dBASE on a search-and-replace mission, you need to fill out all of the same information you used for Edit⇨Search⇨Find Text including text for Find What, a direction (Up or Down), and decisions about whether dBASE should Match Whole Words only and whether it should Match Case. In addition, you need to enter text in the Replace With box to replace whatever you put into the Find What box. Finally, you need to decide whether you want to move to the first match dBASE can find (with the Find button) or Replace All of the occurrences of the Find What text with the new text. If you've already moved to a match, you also have the choice of using the Replace button to change the selected text and move on to the next match.

More stuff

To make changes to the contents of other fields in your database tables, you need to use Table⇨Replace Records.

Edit⇨Search⇨Top Line

Moves you to the top line of the memo field or program. That's all there is to it.

For keyboard krazies

Just the facts

Just select Edit⇨Search⇨Top Line and, faster than a speeding bullet, you're at the first line of the current memo field or program.

More stuff

To move to a specific line, use Edit⇨Search⇨Go to Line Number. To jump to the last line, use Edit⇨Search⇨Bottom Line.

Edit⇨Select All

Selects everything and I mean everything. OK, maybe not everything, but everything within the current object. If you're in a field, only the text within that field is selected, but if you're working with designing a form, then every control on the form is selected.

Just the facts

This one's real easy. Just go to the menu and select the command. Generally, you use Edit⇨Select All with the commands in the Properties window (such as the background color). Because everything is selected, each control will be changed to the new setting, which is important if you want to give your forms or reports a consistent look.

More stuff

If you want almost everything, you can use Edit⇨Select All and then remove items from the selections by holding down the Shift key and clicking on the item to be removed.

The Properties window is controlled by View⇨Object Properties.

Edit⇨Select Form

Selects the form itself rather than any of the objects on it.

Just the facts

Just select Edit⇨Select Form and the form itself is selected. This is most useful for adjusting the properties of the form. Of course, if you're working with the Object Properties dialog box, you can also just select the form from the drop-down list at the top.

More stuff

REFERENCE

To select everything on the form, but not the form itself, use Edit⇨Select All.

Edit⇨Undo

Saves your bacon when you make a mistake. (For us vegetarians, it saves our tofu, but that's a different story.)

For keyboard krazies

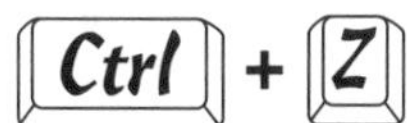

Just the facts

As long as you remember to do it immediately after a mistake, all you need to do is go to the menu and select the command. Or better yet, just use one of the shortcuts.

More stuff

For some reason that is beyond me, Crystal Reports doesn't include an Undo command. This means that you need to be a bit more careful and try not to delete anything until you are absolutely sure you really don't need it.

The actual command name changes to indicate what the last action was (the one that can be undone). Typical command names are Undo Typing, Undo Cut, Undo Paste, and Undo Saved Record.

File⇨Abandon and Close

Tosses out any changes you have made to the form and closes the form. The form is restored to what it looked like the last time you saved your changes.

For keyboard krazies

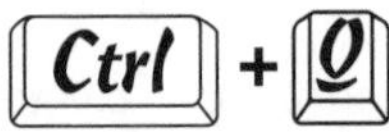

Just the facts

Selecting this command throws out any work that you've done on the form since the last time you saved. That doesn't mean that you are back to where you started, just back to where you last saved.

More stuff

To save the changes on your form, use File⇨Save and Close

File⇨Abandon Record

Clears out any changes to the current field in the current record. It does not reverse all of the changes you've made within the record. As soon as you leave a field, any changes to that field are stored and can no longer be abandoned.

Just the facts

Selecting File⇨Abandon Record is generally the same as selecting Edit⇨Undo. The contents of the current field are returned to whatever they were when you moved to the field.

More stuff

This command is supposed to reverse any and all changes to the current record, but that's not the way it works. It's another one of those dBASE commands that's a great idea, lousy programming.

A slightly more useful command is File⇨Abandon Record and Close.

File⇨Abandon Record and Close

Changes the current field back to its original contents and closes the database table. This is the command you use when you are getting frustrated and just want to give up on the whole thing.

For keyboard krazies

Just the facts

Select File⇨Abandon Record and Close when you don't want to save the changes you just made to the current field and when you are ready to close the current table. This is the same as selecting Edit⇨Undo followed by File⇨Close.

More stuff

The command is supposed to restore the whole record, but it doesn't usually. It's a shame, because it would be a nice feature.

A more useful command is File⇨Save and Close, which saves any changes and closes the table. It works.

File⇨Close

Closes the current window whether it contains a table, a form, or whatever. With most things, if you've made changes that haven't been saved, you are very politely asked about saving the changes before the window is closed. With a table, dBASE just saves the changes and closes the window.

For keyboard krazies

Just the facts

This is an amazingly easy-to-use command. The only thing that might happen is that, if you try to close a window for a report, form, or query in which you haven't saved your changes, you'll be asked about whether or not to save them. If you want to keep the changes, click on Yes. If you want to throw them out (and go back to what you had when you last saved), select No.

More stuff

To close all windows and get out of the program, use File⇨Exit. To just close all of the windows, use Windows⇨Close All Windows.

File⇨Exit

Turns the program off so that you can go home for the day. You are asked about saving any changes before all of the windows are closed.

For keyboard krazies

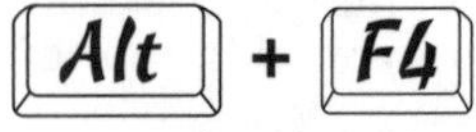

Just the facts

Select File⇨Exit, and dBASE (or Crystal Reports) starts closing down business. If you've made any changes that you haven't saved, you're given a chance to save them.

More stuff

Closing dBASE does not automatically close Crystal Reports; if you've been designing reports, cross-tabs, or labels, you need to close both programs separately.

File⇨Import

Converts a spreadsheet into a database table. dBASE calculates the type and size for each field based upon the information in each column of the spreadsheet.

Just the facts

The first thing to consider is that the new database table is created in the same directory as the spreadsheet. This means that you should move a copy of the spreadsheet to your database directory before importing the spreadsheet into your catalog. When you select File⇨Import, you get a rather simple dialog box with a box for entering the name of the spreadsheet. If you like, you can click on the button to the right (with a little wrench on it) to use a dialog box for selecting the file. Once the file is selected, you can use the Headings check box to let dBASE know whether the first line of the spreadsheet contains field names. (If it does, put a check in the box. If you leave the Headings check box cleared, dBASE creates names for each field. Be warned — dBASE's taste in names runs to the boring and not-very-useful.

More stuff

If you want to use a Paradox or dBASE for DOS table, you should use File⇨Open to open the table directly. To use a table created in another program, you must use the File⇨Save As command in the other program to save the file in either a dBASE or Paradox format.

To import information from other database programs or in other formats, use Table⇨Table Utilities⇨Append Records from File. The best way to export information is to create a simple table report in Crystal Reports and use the File⇨Print⇨File command.

File⇨List of Recent Files

At the bottom of the file menu in dBASE is a list of the last five files you opened. Selecting a file from this list is much easier than using the File⇨Open command to track it down.

Just the facts

The very fact that the most recently used commands are on the File menu is one of the most useful shortcuts in existence (particularly for authors who have to revise the same file over and over again). Alt, F, 1 opens the file used last — that is, the first one on the list.)

More stuff

If the file you want isn't on the list, you need to use File⇨Open.

File⇨New

Creates new things for you. What you can create changes depending on whether you are in a catalog or the Navigator in dBASE or working with Crystal Reports.

For mouse maniacs

An odd button that displays the menu you use to select what type of new item you want (a form, a table, a report, and so on).

Just the facts

Once you select File⇨New, a submenu is displayed where you can select the type of object to create. You get the same choices (shown in the figure) whether you are in the Navigator or in a catalog. That's a bit strange because there are things you can create in the Navigator, but not in a catalog. For more information, see the commands listed on the Navigator menu.

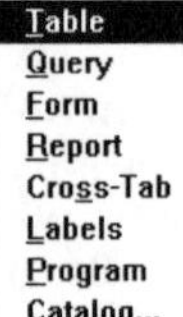

If working in Crystal Reports, you can choose among the three things you can create in Crystal Reports — a Report, Cross-Tab, or Mailing Label.

More stuff

In dBASE, selecting from the New submenu is the same as selecting a type of item and double-clicking on the untitled item.

If you already have a form, report, or query that closely resembles what you want, you don't have to start from scratch to create your new one. Instead, open the one that most resembles what you need and then use File⇨Save As to make a copy with a different name.

File⇨Open

Well, golly, this one opens a file for you. Of course, the key thing is what type of file it opens. And that depends upon where you are when you use the command. Basically, dBASE opens everything, but Crystal Reports opens only reports, labels, and cross-tabs.

For keyboard krazies

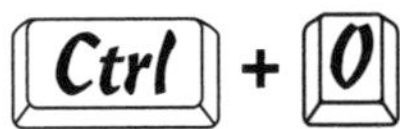

For mouse maniacs

Opens the Open dialog box, which you can use to open a file containing a dBASE item. (I get a bonus each time I say *open*.)

Just the facts

When you select File⇨Open in dBASE, you get what looks like a standard Windows Open File dialog box (which is why there isn't a picture of it). The only difference is that in the lower-right corner is a small section where you can decide exactly how you are opening the file. Based upon the type of item selected in the File Type list, your choices are usually between opening the file to use it (referred to as something like Run Form) or to make changes (something like Design Form). Some types of files (such as catalogs) only offer one choice (such as Open Catalog).

While working with Crystal Reports, you can only open label, report, or cross-tab files, and the file is always opened for design.

More stuff

You should be able to open a report, mailing label, or cross-tab from dBASE and be moved to Crystal Reports. This works fine if Crystal Reports hasn't been opened yet, but if Crystal Reports is already opened, you won't be moved from dBASE. If Crystal Reports is opened and you aren't moved there automatically, hold down the Alt key and repeatedly press Tab until the box in the center of your screen says Crystal Reports. Then let up the Alt key.

In dBASE, you can use the commands within a catalog or the Navigator to open files (see the Catalog and Navigator menu choices). You can also use a catalog (or the Navigator) to create a new file in dBASE, or you can use File⇨New in either dBASE or Crystal Reports.

File⇨Print

Causes the little guys (and gals) with the ink quills inside your computer to start drawing on paper. These scrolls are then rolled very tightly and passed through the wire to your printer where they are straightened out with rollers. On some printers, the individual pages are glued together to form a continuous roll of paper. (Look, it sounds better than "Prints your report, form, or table.")

For keyboard krazies

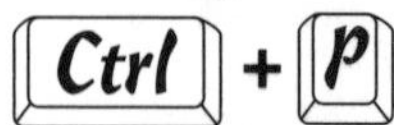

For mouse maniacs

Works the same as selecting File⇨Print — depending upon what is selected, it either opens the Print dialog box or starts printing the document.

Just the facts

What happens when you select the File⇨Print command depends upon what you are printing. If you are printing something designed in Crystal Reports (such as a report or mailing labels), the document just starts printing. For greater control, you need to open the document in Crystal Reports and print it from there.

If you are working with a form, you get a dialog box where you can choose to print All of the records, a group of records you selected before using the command (called appropriately enough, a Selection), or a range of Pages.

With a table, you can choose between printing All of the records, the Rest of the records (starting with the current record), a certain number of records following the current one (the Next few), or a specific Record (by record number).

With both forms and tables, you can select how many copies to print and whether multiple copies are to be collated. You can also select the print quality and whether the information should be stored in a file rather than the printer, but these are advanced topics that are best left alone right now.

More stuff

Generally, it is faster not to collate your copies with Collate Copies. That's because it's faster for your printer to produce several copies once it has the information for page one, rather than waiting for your computer to send each page separately. It's even faster to print one copy and use a copying machine.

When printing records from a table, it is possible to use a *scope expression* to limit which records are printed. A scope expression is similar to a query condition except that you have to include the actual field name in the expression. You can use the Expression Builder to help you create a scope expression. Use a For scope expression to select which records to print. Use a While scope expression to print until the expression is no longer true. You can combine a For scope expression with the All, Next, or Rest options. For example, you can print the next ten records where the State field contains the value WA by putting *State= "WA"* in the For box and *10* in the Next box. In general, you don't combine While with any other option.

To find out about selecting which printer to use and setting the options for your printer, see File⇨Printer Setup. Scope expressions are described in the Glossary.

File⇨Printer Setup

Controls which printer is used and the options for the selected printer.

Just the facts

There are three issues to consider with Printer Setup. First, you have to choose a printer. Second, you have to choose an orientation, either portrait or landscape. Finally, you have to choose the paper size that you are using in your printer. You do all this by using the dialog box shown here.

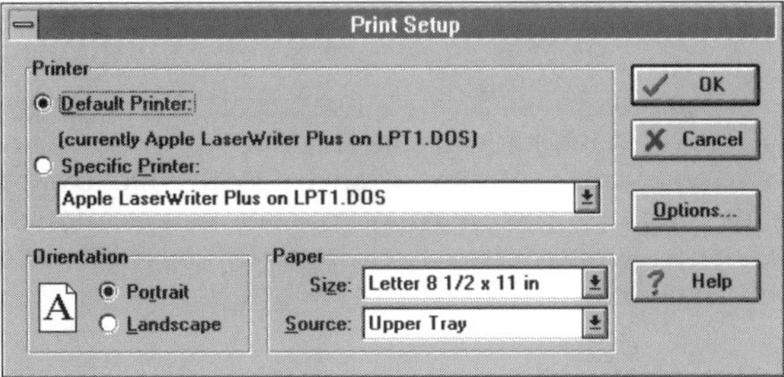

dBASE saves the information in Printer Setup, so you usually only have to worry about getting things right the first time. After that, the settings should probably stay the same — at least until you buy that new laser printer you've been eyeing.

More stuff

The Print Setup dialog box is also available from within dBASE by using the Setup button on the Print dialog box. By the way, the dialog boxes you get when you click on the Options button are different depending upon which printer you are using. These features are controlled by Windows and not dBASE.

dBASE does not offer a command for setting the page margins for your document.

File⇨Save

Stores the current document on disk. If the document already has a name, that name is used. If the document doesn't have a name yet (which means it's never been saved), you are asked to provide a location on your disk for the file in addition to giving it a name.

For keyboard krazies

Ctrl + S

For mouse maniacs

Saves whatever you are currently working on. Use this button often. Don't worry — it won't wear out.

Just the facts

When you select File⇨Save (or use one of the shortcuts), any changes you have made to your document are immediately stored on your disk. It's important to save frequently to avoid accidentally losing work. When your computer is turned off (say because someone tripped over the cord), any work that hasn't been saved is lost.

More stuff

With a database program, you are actually not too likely to lose the information in your database. dBASE saves any changes you make to an entry in your records as soon as you leave the field. In other words, to save the changes to the contents of a field, you can click the mouse somewhere else or press Return, Tab, or any other key that moves you to a different location.

Use File⇨Save As to change the name, location, or format of a file.

File⇨Save and Close

Saves any changes to the form you are working with and then closes the Form Designer. This is useful when you are done making changes and want to move to something else.

For keyboard krazies

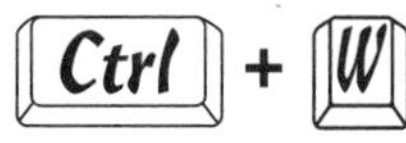

Just the facts

It couldn't be much easier to use. If you've already saved the file (which means it already has a name), select File⇨Save and Close and you're done. The Form Designer closes, and all of your changes are safely stored away. If you haven't yet saved the file, select File⇨Save and Close, enter a name (and optionally select a location), and click OK. You've named your form, stored your changes, and closed the Form Designer with one easy-to-use command.

More stuff

You should use File⇨Save to save a copy of your work occasionally while you are making changes.

File⇨Save As

Gives you the option of changing the name, location, or format of the file you are working with. This can be particularly useful when you want to make changes to a copy of a file rather than to the original, or when you want to store the contents so that they can be used by another program.

For mouse maniacs

If you've never saved the item you are working with, this button works like File⇨Save As. After you've saved the file once, it works like File⇨Save.

Just the facts

When you select File⇨Save As, you get the Save As dialog box where you can enter the name you want to use for the file in the File Name box, select the location using the Drive and Directory lists, and set the File Type by selecting from the list. After making all of your decisions, simply click OK and you're done.

More stuff

Actually, there is no need to use File⇨Save As unless you are making a copy or changing the format — use File⇨Save instead.

File⇨Save Record

Even though you may think you need to use this command to save any changes to the current record, it actually only saves changes to the current field. That's because any other changes were already saved when you moved from one field to another.

For keyboard krazies

Ctrl + S

Just the facts

You can either select File⇨Save Record or just move to another location in your table. Either saves any changes you have made. Personally, I think it's a lot easier to just move to another location.

More stuff

If it worked, File⇨Abandon Record would let you throw out any changes to the record, but it actually only throws out changes to the current field. Still, it is a closely related command.

File⇨Save Record and Close

Closes the current table and saves any changes. Oddly enough, File⇨Close appears to do the exact same thing.

For keyboard krazies

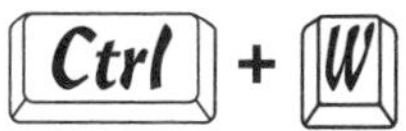

Just the facts

Select the command (or its shortcut) and the table is closed. You can be confident that all of the changes have been safely saved.

More stuff

Any changes you make to a field are automatically saved when you leave that field. In other words, the easiest way to save your changes is just to move to a new location. Of course, I suppose that since you have to use a command to close the window anyway, you might as well use this one.

File⇨Setup Custom Controls

Adds a new tool to the Controls window. You can then use the tool to add the new custom control to your forms. A few samples are included with dBASE, and you'll soon be able to buy entire libraries of these little tools.

Just the facts

File⇨Setup Custom Controls is actually very easy to use. Select the command and then find the file you want to add by using the dialog box. The only thing you need to know is what type of file you are looking for. Probably the most common are VBXs, which are controls created originally for use with Visual Basic. To find these files, select *.VBX from the File Type list. Of course, Borland will probably distribute its own controls as dBASE Custom Controls, which means you will need to use *.CC in the File Type list to see them. Once you find your file, select the file and then select OK (or just double-click on the file).

More stuff

I know they pay me the big bucks to answer all of your questions, but I admit dBASE has me stumped. I can't find any way to remove the control once you've added it. Well, that's not totally true, since I know how to remove the file from your disk, which ensures that it's not going to be used for anything (see Edit⇨Delete). On one level, I refuse to believe Borland could be this sloppy; on the other hand, I'm not thrilled with the idea that I can't find the solution if it exists. That's why this is a warning. Something's wrong, and you need to know about it.

You can also add controls from the Navigator by using Navigator⇨Load Custom Controls.

Form Commands

See the Table commands for an explanation of each command on the Form menu. For example, to learn how to use Form⇨Add Records, see Table⇨Add Records.

Help⇨About dBASE 5.0 for Windows

Particularly useful if you've forgotten what program you are using. The dialog box also lists how much memory is available within your Windows environment, as well as the percentage of resources still available. (Resources are a special portion of memory used by Windows programs to store information about themselves.) If you run out of either memory or resources, you can't open any new documents or programs.

Help⇨Contents

Opens the Help system with the table of contents for the dBASE Help file. From there, you can choose to get more information about dBASE Basics, programming with dBASE, dBASE shortcuts, and how to use the menus and tools that make up dBASE. You also get a Glossary and list of error messages.

For keyboard krazies

Shift + F1

Just the facts

When you're at the Help contents page, you have a couple of choices. The most common approach is to browse your way through the Help system by clicking on one of the underlined, green topics. The first topic, Basics, is generally the most useful, but don't overlook Views and Tools or Keyboard Shortcuts.

Each Help screen contains more underlined, green topics, which you can use to move through the information. In addition, many pages include a "see also" entry at the top that opens a box containing a list of related topics. You'll also find various terms marked with a dotted underline. These words are in the Glossary, and clicking on them reveals a short definition. Or, you can select the Glossary from the main screen.

The Debugger and Language Reference topics are intended for programmers and are really not too useful for the average person. Finally, let's hope that you never have to use any of the topics covered in Error Messages. The only reason you'd end up there is if something isn't working. Of course, if you do run into a problem, this is a good place to look because it lists not only the message but suggested solutions as well.

More stuff

Most of the time, you can get to the topic you need faster by starting the task and then pressing F1. F1 activates context-sensitive help, which means that the Help system tries to guess what you're having problems with and moves to a related Help entry.

To find out more about using the Help system, see Chapter 7 in *dBASE For Windows For Dummies*.

To have dBASE ask you questions and build your form in response to your answers, use Help⇨Experts⇨Form Expert. For help with other tasks, see Help⇨Interactive Tutors.

Help⇨Experts⇨Form Expert

There's really no reason for this to be called the *Experts* command. In fact, it really doesn't make any sense because Experts are designed to help beginners learn new tasks, and besides, there is only one — Form Expert.

For mouse maniacs

Use this button to get some help!

Just the facts

When you select Help⇨Experts⇨Form Expert, you are presented with a dialog box that gives you the choice between creating a blank form or using the Expert. Either choice gives you a new form, but the Expert guides you through the steps of adding the fields and controls that make your form worthwhile. In fact, you just answer questions and the Form Expert does all of the work for you. For more information, see Catalog⇨New Form.

More stuff

For help working through other topics, see Help⇨Interactive Tutors.

Help⇨How to Use Help

It's a nice feeling to know that you can get help even about how to use Help. Select Help⇨How to Use Help, and you see a list of topics of common things you can do in Help, followed by a list of all the Help menus. Just click on whichever topic you want to learn more about, and you're on your way to mastering the Help system. Click on Help Basics for a quick introduction to how to move through a Help file.

Help⇨Interactive Tutors

A baker's dozen of topics that can be used to get help with most of the common tasks within dBASE. With an Interactive Tutor, dBASE opens a special window over your database, which gives you step-by-step instructions for performing the task. It's kinda like having your office guru stand over your shoulder and try to help. Fortunately for me, the IDG ...*For Dummies* books are much friendlier.

For mouse maniacs

This button gets you a tutor.

Just the facts

When you first select Help⇨Interactive Tutors (or click on the Tutors' button), you see the dialog box shown here. If you select one of the main topics on the left, you see the various subtopics in that category on the right.

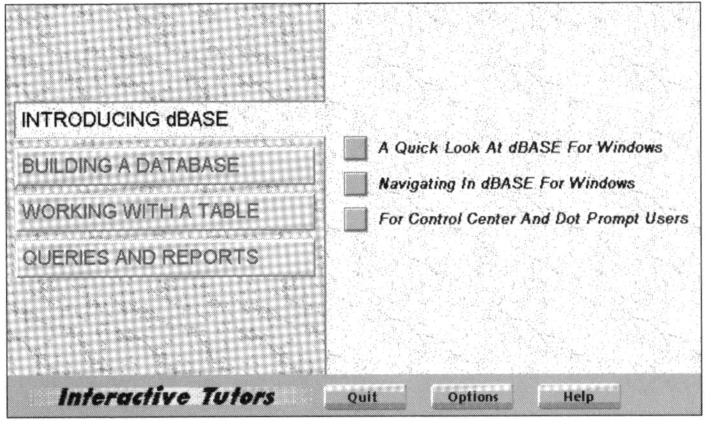

When you select one of the subtopics (by clicking on it), the appropriate tutor starts up. You move through the screen of the tutorial by using buttons on the bottom of the screen. The most important thing to remember is that the button with a red X is used to take you back to the opening Interactive Tutors screen. From the opening screen, you can click on Quit to stop using the tutors.

Each tutor covers a different aspect of using dBASE, starting with a very basic tour of the screen and moving through designing your own tables and queries. With many of the tutors, you have a choice of working with sample data provided by dBASE or your own information. That way, if you are still learning to do something, you can start up the tutor to help you through the steps using your own work.

More stuff

For more on using the Interactive Tutors, see Chapter 7 in *dBASE For Windows For Dummies*.

If you are creating a form, you can use Help⇨Experts⇨Form Expert to have dBASE ask you questions about what you want and to create the form for you based upon your answers.

Help⇨Keyboard

Lists all of the keyboard shortcuts available within dBASE. Of course, this quick reference does the same thing, so you probably will never need to use this command. I suppose there is some slight advantage to the fact that it's on the screen for you.

Just the facts

When you select Help⇨Keyboard, you are taken to the Keyboard Shortcuts topic within the dBASE Help system. You can then select from the topics shown to see a list of shortcuts for a particular part of the program. For example System-wide Keystrokes are ones that work no matter where you are in dBASE, while Text Editing Keystrokes only work when you are working within a Text Editor window.

More stuff

Although it's fastest if you learn the various shortcuts for the commands, you can also learn some techniques that make using the keyboard easier. For example, when selecting commands from a menu with the keyboard, you don't need to hold down the Alt key while you type the letter to open the menu. This can help reduce the strain on your hands and wrists while using the program. In other words, instead of holding down the Alt key and pressing F to open the File menu, you can press Alt, release it, and then press F.

Help⇨Language

Explains all of the nuances of the dBASE programming language. In order for this to be useful to you, you need to know how to program in dBASE. Each of the commands is listed with a description and examples of how to use it. There are several indexes to the commands, including an alphabetical listing of the commands and one that groups the commands into categories based upon what each command does.

Help⇨Search

Tracks down any topics that are listed with the words you enter. For example, all the menu commands can be found by entering the actual command name.

Just the facts

After you open the Search dialog box (either by selecting Help⇨Search or by clicking the Search button from within Help), you are presented with the dialog box shown here. Notice the unlabeled text box in the upper-left. That's where you enter what you're looking for.

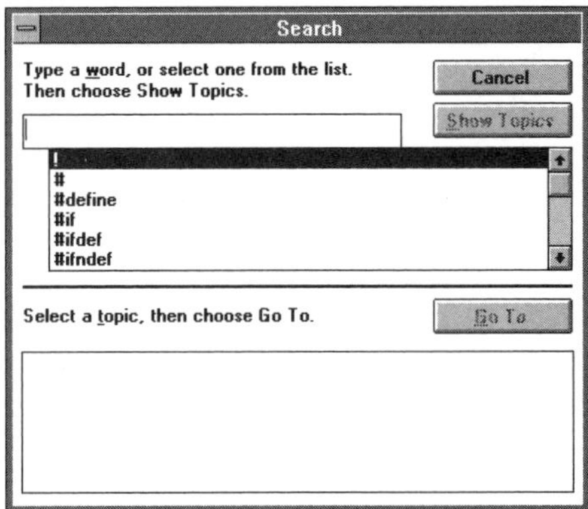

Start typing either a word or phrase that describes what you are looking for. As you type, the Help system displays the closest matching phrase. If none of the suggested phrases is quite what you need, try deleting what you've typed and using a different phrase.

When you find a phrase that seems to describe what you want, click on the Show Topics button, which will list all of the Help entries that are associated with that phrase. Look through the list for the one that seems closest and click on it. You'll find that the topics listed are generally related and that you can move between them. You can also select the Search button from any topic, and it will return you to the list you started from.

More stuff

Once you've entered your search words and a likely topic appears on the list, you can just double-click on the topic to display all of the Help entries. Then double-click on the entry you want to see to open it.

Help⇨Views and Tools

Provides examples of all the various SpeedBars, menus, and windows available within dBASE. Each example is neatly labeled so that you learn how to use each part.

Just the facts

Views and Tools section of the Help system is designed to help you learn how to use dBASE efficiently by learning all of the tools

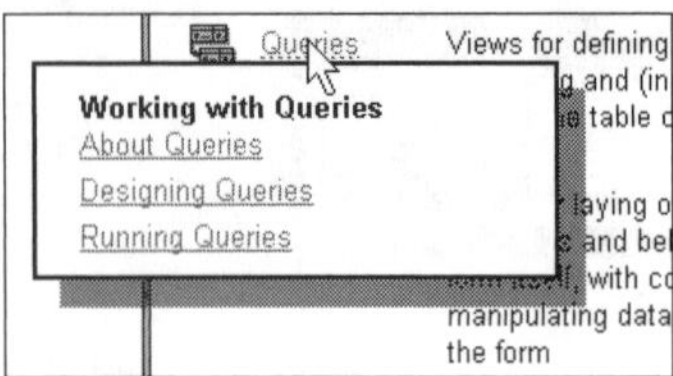

that are available for you on the screen. Select Help⇨Views and Tools to see the opening screen for the section. The most useful topics are toward the bottom of the screen where each type of dBASE item has an entry (Tables, Queries, Forms, and so on). When you select one of these entries, you get a small pop-up window with some topic choices. The figure here shows the choices for the Queries entry.

For a general overview, select the first entry (in this case, About Queries). Each of the other topics covers one of ways in which you can work with that item (in the example here, Designing Queries or Running Queries). When you select one of these topics, you are taken to a page that has topics for a general overview, common tasks within that topic, and entries for descriptions of the associated menus, SpeedBar, and SpeedMenu. (The SpeedMenu is the menu that appears if you click the right mouse button.) If there is a topic labeled Design Surface (or something similar), select it to see an example of the window where you perform the tasks.

More stuff

If you are looking for information about using a single command, it's generally faster to use Help⇨Search. For help with command tasks, check out Help⇨Interactive Tutors or, if you want to create a form, Help⇨Experts⇨Form Expert.

Label⇨Bottom Page

Talk about your misnamed commands. You might think that this takes you to the bottom of a page of labels, but instead it takes you to the last page of labels.

For keyboard krazies

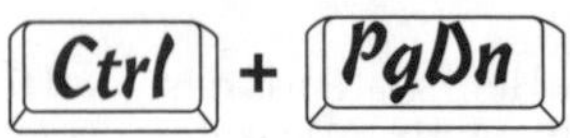

For mouse maniacs

Jumps to the last page in the current document of labels. It looks somewhat like a fast forward button.

Just the facts

When you select Label⇨Bottom Page, you jump to the last page of labels in the current document. If you want to move around on the current page of labels, use the scroll bars along the bottom edge or the right side of the document window.

More stuff

You can move to the other locations within the file using Label⇨Next Page, Label⇨Previous Page, and Label⇨Top Page (which takes you to the first page, not the top of the current page).

Label⇨Next Page

Moves you one page forward in the current document of labels.

For keyboard krazies

For mouse maniacs

Moves you to the next page of labels.

Just the facts

Select Label⇨Next Page (or use one of the shortcuts) and you'll find yourself on the next page of labels. To move around on the current page, use the scroll bars at the end of the window.

More stuff

You can also use Label⇨Bottom Page to go to the last page, Label⇨Previous Page to move back a page, and Label⇨Top Page to jump to the first page.

Label⇨Previous Page

Takes you to the previous page of labels in the current document.

For keyboard krazies

For mouse maniacs

Takes you back to the previous page of labels.

Just the facts

Select Label⇨Previous Page and you are moved back a single page within the current set of labels.

More stuff

Label⇨Bottom Page moves to the last page, Label⇨Next Page moves forward a page, and Label⇨Top Page jumps to the first page.

Label⇨Top Page

Jumps to the first page of labels in the current document (not to the top of the current page, as you might think based on the name).

For keyboard krazies

For mouse maniacs

Jumps to the first page of labels in the current document.

Just the facts

If you want to move to the first page of labels in the current document, select Label⇨Top Page or any of its shortcuts. Use the scroll bars to move around on the current page of labels.

More stuff

Other shortcuts include using Label⇨Next Page to go forward a page, Label⇨Previous Page to move back a page, and Label⇨Bottom to jump to the last page.

Layout⇨Align Bottom

Arranges all of the selected controls (including any fields or text) so that the bottom edges are along a straight line.

For mouse maniacs

Causes all the selected controls to line up along the bottom edge.

Just the facts

First, you need to select the group of controls that you want to align. You can do this in two ways. One way is to click on the first item, and then hold down the Shift key and click on additional items to add them to the group. The second method is to draw a selection rectangle around the controls. To draw a selection rectangle, move the cursor so that it is positioned over the form's background to the upper-left of the controls you want to include in the group. Then, hold down the mouse button and drag to the lower-right. Any control that is enclosed by or touched by the selection rectangle is selected when you release the mouse button. (Left-handed folk may find it easier to drag from the upper-left to the lower-right). If you want to remove a control from the group, hold down the Shift key and click on the control to be removed.

After you select the items, you can select Layout⇨Align Bottom to move the controls. dBASE locates the control with an edge closest to the bottom of the form (the lowest edge) and moves all of the other controls so that their bottom edges are on the same line as the lowest edge.

More stuff

Use Layout⇨Align Left, Layout⇨Align Right, or Layout⇨Align Top to align other edges of the controls. If you want to align controls using their centers, use Layout⇨Align Special.

Layout⇨Align Left

Moves the selected controls so that they are lined up along their left edges. The controls are moved so that they are in line with the edge at the far left (closest to the left edge of the form).

For mouse maniacs

Moves all the selected controls so that their left edges are aligned.

Just the facts

Select the controls to be moved either by drawing a selection rectangle around them or by holding down the Shift key and clicking on items to add them to the group. When drawing a selection rectangle, be sure to start on the form's background rather than on one of the controls. You can remove an item from the group by holding down the Shift key and clicking on the control to be removed. To determine where the controls will be placed, find the control with its left edge closest to the left edge of the form. Select Layout⇨Align Left and all of the other controls are moved so that their left edges are in line with the left edge of that control.

More stuff

Layout⇨Align Bottom, Layout⇨Align Right, or Layout⇨Align Top can be used to align other edges of the controls. Layout⇨Align Special aligns controls based upon their centers.

Layout⇨Align Right

Moves all of the selected controls so that they are lined up with whichever edge is closest to the right side of the form.

For mouse maniacs

Arranges the controls so that their right edges are neatly lined up.

Just the facts

To select the controls that you want to move, you can either hold down the Shift key and click on items to add them to the group, or position the cursor over the form's background and drag to form a rectangle around the items to be selected. (Any controls touched by the rectangle will be included in the selection.) Once your group is selected, select Layout⇨Align Right to move the controls. dBASE locates the edge within the selected controls that is closest to the right side of the form and moves all of the other controls so that their right edges are aligned with that edge.

More stuff

To remove a control from the group, hold down the Shift key and click on it.

Layout⇨Align Left, Layout⇨Align Bottom, or Layout⇨Align Top align controls using the other edges. If you want to align controls using their centers, use Layout⇨Align Special.

Layout⇨Align Special

Moves the selected controls so that their centers fall along the same line (either horizontal or vertical).

Just the facts

As with the other alignment commands on the Layout menu, you need to select the controls to be moved. The easiest way to do this is to position your cursor over the form's background and drag a selection rectangle around the controls for the group. You can also add items to a group by holding down the Shift key and clicking on them. If you hold down the Shift key and click on a control that's already part of the group, the control is removed from the group.

The Align Special submenu has two groups of choices. The two horizontal commands move the controls side-to-side so that their centers are all stacked on the same invisible line running up and down the screen. The two vertical commands arrange the controls so that the centers are on the same line across the screen. The vertical commands move the controls up and down on the screen. The absolute commands (Absolute Horizontal Center and Absolute Vertical Center) position the items in the center of the form. The two relative commands (Relative Horizontal Center and Relative Vertical Center) determine the center of the selected group and move the controls in line with that position.

More stuff

Use Layout⇨Align Bottom, Layout⇨Align Left, Layout⇨Align Right, or Layout⇨Align Top to align controls using their edges.

Layout⇨Align Top

Arranges the controls so that they are all lined up with the edge within the group that is closest to the top of the form.

For mouse maniacs

Moves the controls so that the top edge of each control is on the same invisible line.

Just the facts

First, you need to get all of the items you want to move into a single group. One method is to hold down the Shift key while you click on each item. Another approach is to position the cursor over the background of the form and drag the cursor so that it forms a rectangle around all of the controls you want in the group. Holding down the Shift key and clicking on a selected control removes it from the group.

To find out where the controls will be positioned, look at the controls within the group and find the edge closest to the top of the form. When you select Layout⇨Align Top, all of the controls are moved so that their top edges are the same distance from the top edge of the form.

More stuff

You can use Layout⇨Align Left, Layout⇨Align Right, or Layout⇨Align Bottom to align controls using one of the other edges. If you want to use the controls' centers for alignment, use Layout⇨Align Special.

Layout➪Bring Closer

Each control on the form exists within its own layer. The order of the layers determines which controls appear to be on top of other controls. Layout➪Bring Closer moves the selected control one layer closer to the viewer (toward the top of the stack of controls).

For mouse maniacs

Moves the selected control or controls closer to the viewer, which can cause parts of other controls to be hidden.

Just the facts

The look of your form is determined by the position of the control on the form in three dimensions — left to right, top to bottom, and front to back. Controls that are closer to the front are seen as being on top of controls that are toward the back. To move a control closer to the viewer (so that it can cover other controls), select the control and then select Layout➪Bring Closer.

More stuff

If a control is completely hiding another control, the only way to get to the hidden control is by sending the first farther away until it no longer is covering the second control. Often, it will be easiest to send the first control all the way to the back (with Layout➪Send to Back) and then rearrange the order.

You can select a group of controls and move them together using Layout➪Bring Closer. The order of the controls within the group remains unchanged.

The easiest way to put a group of controls in order is to select the one you want on top and then send it to the back. Next, select the control to be on the second layer and send it to the back (behind the one you just moved). Continue this process until you've moved all the controls into the order that you want.

The Layout➪Bring Closer, Layout➪Bring to Front, Layout➪Send Farther, and Layout➪Send to Back commands are used to position the controls on the form from front to back. Use the Layout➪Align commands to position the controls in the other two dimensions.

Layout⇨Bring to Front

Causes that object to jump to the top of the stack (so that it appears on top of all other controls and closest to the viewer). Any other objects in the same area of the screen will be partially or completely hidden.

For mouse maniacs

Moves the selected control(s) to the very front so that any other controls appear behind it.

Just the facts

Because each control exists on its own layer, you can move each control within the stack to reveal or cover other controls. Selecting a control and then selecting Layout⇨Bring to Front moves the control so that it is at the top of the stack and therefore not covered by any other controls.

More stuff

Layout⇨Bring to Front also works with a group of controls. Just select the group before selecting the command. The entire group is moved to the front, and the order of the controls within the group remains unchanged.

Layout⇨Bring Closer, Layout⇨Send Farther, and Layout⇨Send to Back are also used to position the controls on the form from front to back.

Layout⇨Send Farther

Moves the control one layer further from the viewer (toward the bottom of the stack).

For mouse maniacs

Causes the selected control or controls to appear farther away from the viewer, which may move the selected control(s) behind other controls.

Just the facts

Select the control and then select Layout⇨Send Farther to move the control back one layer. Each control has its own layer, and the order of the layers within the stack determines which controls appear to be on top and therefore closer to the viewer.

More stuff

Like the other commands that change the order of layers, Layout⇨Send Farther can be used to move a group of controls without changing the order of the layers within the group.

Use Layout⇨Bring Closer or Layout⇨Bring to Front to move controls closer to the viewer. Layout⇨Send to Back moves the control to the bottom of the stack (so that everything else appears on top of it).

Layout⇨Send to Back

Causes the selected control to move to the bottom of the stack (farthest away from the viewer), where it will be partially or completely covered by other objects in the same area.

For mouse maniacs

Moves the selected controls so that they are at the bottom of the stack, and any other controls appear in front of, or on top of, them.

Just the facts

Each control is on its own layer, and the order of the layers determines which controls cover up other controls. A control that is sent to the back can be covered up by any other control on the screen. To move a control to the back, select it and then select Layout⇨Send to Back.

More stuff

You may need to move an object several times to reveal another object that is being hidden. Imagine that you have four objects, conveniently labeled Object-1, Object-2, Object-3, and Object-4, with Object-1 being closest to the viewer and the others in order toward the back (with Object-4 being the farthest from the viewer). Now, part of Object-1 is covering up part of Object-3, and you need to fix it. You select Object-1 and then select

Layout⇨Send to Back. The objects are now, from front to back, Object-2, Object-1, Object-3, and Object-4. Unfortunately, your problem hasn't gone away because Object-1 is still in front of Object-3. Fortunately, selecting Layout⇨Send to Back again (with Object-1 still selected) solves your problem.

You can move a group of controls to the back by selecting the group and then selecting Layout⇨Send to Back. The order of the controls within the group will not be changed.

Use Layout⇨Bring Closer, Layout⇨Bring to Front, Layout⇨Send Farther, and Layout⇨Send to Back to position the controls on the form from front to back.

Layout⇨Tools⇨Design Menu

Opens the Menu Designer, which is used to create any special menus that are to be displayed with the form. You can also use the Menu Designer to hide the standard menus. This command is only used when you are creating your own dBASE applications, which requires extensive programming and is beyond what I'm going to cover in this book. Just so you know, if you get into the Menu Designer, you can select File⇨Close to get back to your form.

Layout⇨Tools⇨Design Query

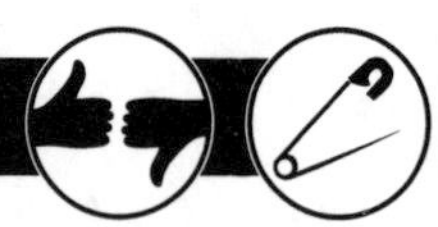

Creates a new query just as if you had used Catalog⇨New Query (where the details are described), or File⇨New⇨Query, or any of the other commands for creating a query. After you create your query, you need to select it as the form's view. To do this, first save the query and then move to the form selecting a control (any control) and opening the control's DataLink property (by clicking on the button with the wrench, at the left); select the View button in the dialog box that appears and then select the new query.

Menu Commands

Yes, there actually is a menu called Menu. The commands on it are used to design menus to go with your forms but are a bit too complex to be covered in a quick reference. Your office guru gets paid to deal with these sorts of commands and, depending on her or his personality, may really enjoy it. However, I'm confident that a nice person like you would never be involved with the likes of menu design.

Navigator Commands

Most of the commands on the Navigator menu are the same as those on the Catalog menu. Because I believe that you should use catalogs to organize your database files and that it's not worth wasting the paper to describe each of the commands twice, you'll find the commands for working with table, report, form, label, query, and program items discussed under the corresponding catalog command. In other words, Navigator⇨New Table is discussed under Catalog⇨New Table.

The only difference is that the commands on the Navigator menu work with any item in the current directory (or, optionally, along the search path), whereas the catalog items only work with items within the current catalog. However, when you create a new item within a catalog, the file for it is created in the current directory and is available from the Navigator (unless you insist upon putting it somewhere else).

Because you cannot put an image, sound, catalog, or custom control into a catalog, the commands for those items are discussed near here under the proper Navigator command.

Navigator⇨Design Image

Opens the selected image in your graphics program so that you can make changes. It doesn't matter what you used to create the image; dBASE generally opens Microsoft Paintbrush for image files.

For keyboard krazies

Shift + F2

For mouse maniacs

Yes, this is the same button you use to design everything else. To design an image, make sure you have an image selected.

Just the facts

If you have an image file selected (one that has an extension of BMP or PCX), selecting Navigator⇨Design Image opens Microsoft Paintbrush, which you can use to make changes to the image. Paintbrush runs as a separate program, and you need to remember to use File⇨Save within Paintbrush to save your changes.

More stuff

The simplest way to insert image files into your database tables is by creating a field of the type *binary.* When you double-click an empty binary field (like the one shown in the following figure), you are presented with a dialog box with a choice for the Image Viewer or the Sound Player.

To add an image, select the Image Viewer and then select File⇨Insert From File. Locate the file containing the image and double-click it. This places the image into the Image Viewer and into the field. Close the Image Viewer window to return to your table. The field now contains an image icon (like the one shown here).

To open the Image Viewer and display the image when working with the table, simply double-click the image icon.

You can also insert images into OLE fields using the Edit⇨Insert Object or Edit⇨Paste Link commands in the OLE Viewer window. To open the OLE Viewer, double-click an OLE field.

Navigator⇨Design Sound

Opens the Sound Recorder installed by your soundboard software. If you don't have a soundboard installed on your computer, you generally cannot create or use sounds with your database.

For keyboard krazies

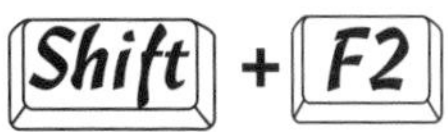

For mouse maniacs

Select the sound file you want to work with and then click the button to work with the file in the Sound Recorder (or whatever software your system uses).

Just the facts

Select the sound file you want to work with and then select Navigator⇨Design Sound. The sound is opened in an editing program where you can usually record a new sound or change the contents of the recording. The exact utility used for the recording depends on the way your system is set up.

More stuff

To insert a sound into your database, follow the same steps as for inserting an image (as described in the note in the More stuff section for Navigator⇨Design Image) except, instead of using the Image Viewer, use the Sound Player. The icon for a field containing a sound looks like the one shown here.

As with images, you can also insert a sound into an OLE field, but a binary field is generally easier to work with and works as well.

Navigator⇨Display Image

Opens the selected image in the Image Viewer so that you can see what's inside the file. See the pretty picture!

For keyboard krazies

For mouse maniacs

Select an image, click the button, and sit back to admire the sights.

Just the facts

All you need to do is select the image file you want to view and select Navigator⇨Display Image. The Image Viewer window opens with the image already loaded. You can change the size and shape of the Image Viewer window to change the size and shape of the displayed image.

More stuff

If you want to display an image that is already stored in a database table, just double-click the field containing the image to open the Image Viewer.

For information about how to add images to your database tables, see Navigator⇨Design Image.

Navigator⇨Load Custom Controls

Adds the selected custom control to the tools available when designing a form. Once you have added a custom control, you can use it on any of your forms.

For keyboard krazies

For mouse maniacs

You have to first display the available controls and select one in order to use this button.

Just the facts

The first thing you have to do is display the available custom controls. To do that, select the Custom icon with the Navigator and then, in the Custom Files text box, enter an asterisk followed by the extension for the type of custom control you want. For example, enter ***.VBX** to view any Visual Basic controls and ***.CC** to view any dBASE Custom Controls. You may enter more than one description if you separate them with commas. To see both Visual Basic controls and dBASE Custom Controls, enter ***.VBX, *.CC** in the Custom Files text box. Press Enter to display all matching files in the current directory. To move to a different directory, click the folder icon next to the Current Directory TextBox at the top of the Navigator.

Once you locate the control you want to add, click it and then select Navigator⇨Load Custom Controls. The control is added to your form tools.

More stuff

There is no easy way to remove a control once it has been added.

Once you've loaded a particular control, you don't need to continue displaying the controls within the Navigator. In fact, you can change directories or display a different group of files using the Custom Files box without changing the loaded custom controls.

You can also use File⇨Setup Custom Controls to load a control for use with your forms.

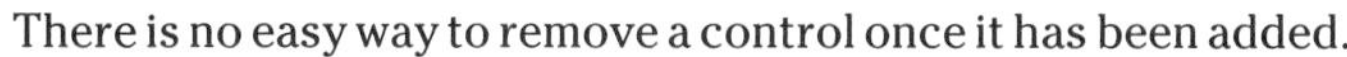

Navigator⇨New Catalog

Creates a new catalog that you can then use to organize all your related dBASE files. The most important thing to understand is that a catalog is an organizational group: an item can belong to several different catalogs, and some items won't belong to any catalog.

For keyboard krazies

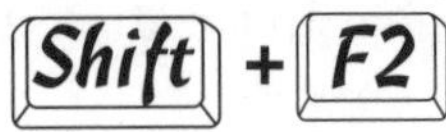

For mouse maniacs

Gives you a new catalog when an untitled catalog item is selected.

Just the facts

If you continue to develop databases with dBASE, finding a single file among all the files you have accumulated may become difficult. You can avoid this problem by using catalogs to group your related files.

To create a new catalog, start in the Navigator window and select the untitled catalog item. Then select Navigator⇨New Catalog to open the Create Catalog dialog box (which looks suspiciously like a Save As dialog box). Alternatively, you can just double-click the untitled catalog item.

Next, select a location for the catalog using the Directory and Drive lists and enter a name for the catalog. Once you've decided what to call your catalog and where to put it, you can select OK.

In the Catalog Item Description dialog box that comes up, enter a short description of what the catalog will be used for (for example, **Contains database examples for book**). When you click OK, you return to the window for your new catalog, which you can now fill with all your database items.

More stuff

Some types of items (such as images, sounds, custom controls, and other catalogs) cannot be stored within a catalog. The files for these items can only be accessed from the Navigator.

Find out more about catalogs in Chapter 2 of *dBASE For Windows For Dummies*.

To add items to a catalog, either drag them from the Navigator onto the catalog window or use Catalog⇨Add Item. To remove a catalog, select it in the Navigator and use Edit⇨Delete.

Navigator⇨New Image

Opens Paintbrush so that you can create a new image. What you do inside of Paintbrush is a personal decision and not something that is discussed in this quick reference. To find out how to use an image, see Navigator⇨Design Image.

For keyboard krazies

Shift + F2

For mouse maniacs

Opens Paintbrush when you have an untitled image item selected.

Just the facts

The facts are that there's nothing more to be said. Well, one tip is that you can just double-click the untitled image item. For more about Paintbrush, read IDG's *Windows For Dummies* by Andy Rathbone.

Navigator⇨New Sound

Opens the Sound Recorder (or whatever software is used by your soundboard) so that you can record new sounds. You have to select the untitled sound item and have a soundboard and microphone on your system in order to use this command effectively. For more information about working with sounds, see Navigator⇨Design Sound.

For keyboard krazies

Shift + F2

For mouse maniacs

Select the untitled sound item and click the button to start recording your top ten hit (or something more useful for your database).

Just the facts

Exactly how you create a new sound using the software on your system depends on what you have installed. The soundboard and its software are separate from dBASE. Once you select the untitled sound item and then Navigator⇨New Sound (or just double-click the untitled sound item), you're in a different world (or at least a different program).

Navigator⇨Open Catalog

Opens the selected catalog so that you can see what items are grouped inside it. You can get the same effect by double-clicking the catalog item.

For keyboard krazies

For mouse maniacs

When you have a catalog item selected, this button opens it.

Just the facts

Select the catalog you want to work with and then Navigator⇨Open Catalog. After that, you need to use the commands on the Catalog menu to work with the items.

More stuff

REFERENCE

The various commands on the Catalog menu are used to work with items in the catalog itself.

Navigator⇨Play Sound

Plays the selected sound without bothering to open a separate window. This can be particularly useful if you're lonely and want your computer to talk to you (or if you're trying to figure out which file contains which sound).

For keyboard krazies

For mouse maniacs

Select the sound item and then press the button; your computer will start making sounds at you.

Just the facts

There's really not much to this command. You select the sound item and then you select Navigator⇨Play Sound (or one of the shortcuts) and your computer makes noises. Actually, just double-clicking the sound item is easier, but the choice is yours.

More stuff

To play a sound that is stored within a database field, double-click the sound icon (a little musical note). For more information, see Navigator⇨Design Sound.

Navigator⇨Refresh Items

Updates the items listed within the Navigator. An updated list is very useful if you delete files using another program or if you are working on a network where someone else may have added or deleted files.

Just the facts

Select Navigator⇨Refresh Items to have the Navigator check which files are currently available in the selected directory and update the list to match. This command is particularly important if you are having trouble getting any of the files listed to open — it may be that the file has been deleted and no one has bothered to tell dBASE. When you refresh the list, you get the most current information. If you keep having problems, take those Twinkies and bribe the office guru.

More stuff

Use the Current Directory box (and the folder button next to it) to select the directory to be used.

Procedure Commands

When you're working with a form, these commands appear to let you add instructions for performing special actions when the form is being used. This is called *programming* and is something we try not to talk about in polite company. These commands are all way beyond this book, so you'll need to look elsewhere if you want to learn about them (but why would you want to do that?).

Program Commands

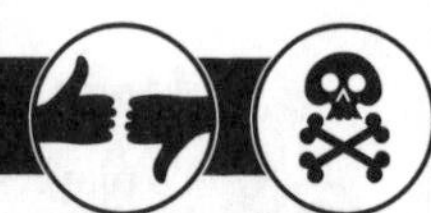

Not surprisingly, these commands appear when you are working with programs. You can use these commands to run your program (make it do whatever your instructions tell it to) or to check your instructions. One of the commands, Debug, opens a separate program with its own set of menus called the dBASE Debugger. Programming and all these commands are way beyond this book, so you'll need to look elsewhere if you want to learn about them (but why would you want to do that?). It's not that they're bad commands; you just don't want to mess with them.

Properties⇨Catalog Window

Sets the properties for the three views available within a catalog window (Large Icons, Small Icons, and Details). The properties are set for all your catalog windows so that each window looks the same.

Just the facts

From a catalog window, select Properties➪Catalog Window to display the Catalog Properties dialog box. Each section in the dialog box controls a different view in a catalog window. For each, you can set the spacing between items (using the X Spacing and Y Spacing boxes). Because the Details view is a list, you can only control the spacing between the lines on the list (the Y Spacing). Select the Reset button for any of the views to use the spacing recommended by the designers of dBASE.

More stuff

To change the view within the current catalog, use View➪Large Icons, View➪Small Icons, or View➪Details.

Properties➪Desktop

Controls a wide variety of settings about the dBASE environment, from the sound of the bell to where dBASE looks for files to how it behaves when you're working with forms and tables.

Just the facts

When you select Properties➪Desktop, you are presented with the dialog box shown here. This is the view if you select the command while viewing a catalog. Notice that the dialog box has several different tabs along the bottom. (Data Entry is selected in the figure.) Depending on what you are doing when you select the command, a different tab may be selected.

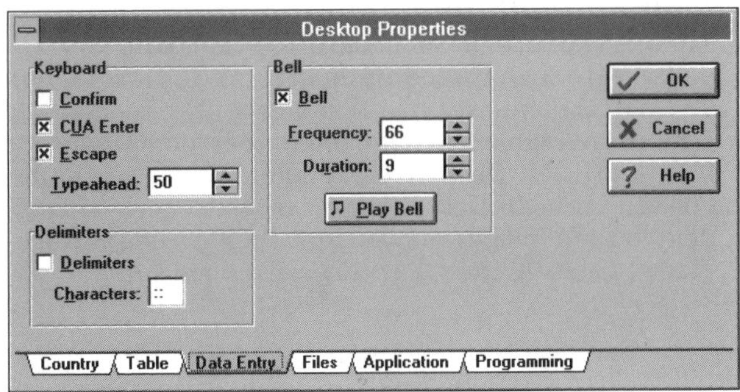

You use the tabs along the bottom of the dialog box to select a category of settings. Each tab displays a different set of choices within the dialog box. For example, selecting Country displays the choices shown here.

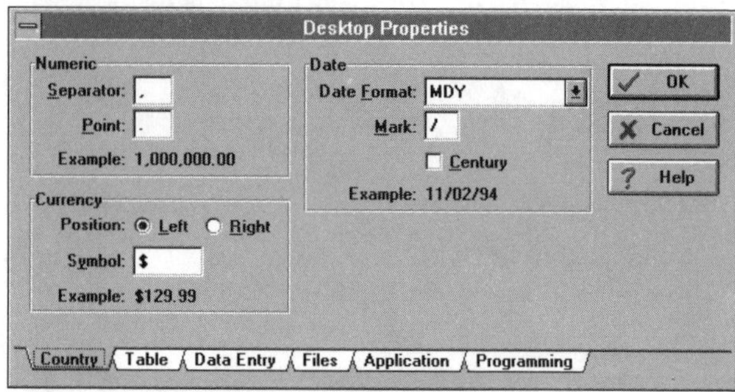

Because so many choices are hidden within this dialog box, I'm not going to attempt to cover them all. I will, however, hit the high points. To find out more about the choices available for a category, click the appropriate tab on the bottom of the dialog box and then select the Help button. dBASE opens the Help system and displays a page describing each of the options currently displayed in the dialog box.

The Country category lets you set the format for numbers, currency, and dates, all of which are easy to use because, as you make changes, the examples change to show you the results. In most cases, you should leave these formats the way they were set when you started using the program. The only exception is if you work with information for more than one country and need to change between the two countries' standards.

The most important command in the Table category is Deleted. If you want to see any records that are marked for deletion but are still in your database table, remove the check mark next to this option. Your table now has a separate column labeled Del at the left edge (just to the right of the column for record number). A check mark in the Del column means the record is marked for deletion and will be removed from the file when you use the Table⇨Table Utilities⇨Pack Records command.

The Autosave option is also potentially important — except dBASE seems to save records automatically whether or not this option is checked. Two other options on this card, Exact and Near, control how dBASE searches for records. If you want to restrict your text searches so that dBASE only returns exact matches and not every instance in which that text appears (if you don't want to get *police* when you're looking for *lice,* for example), check the Exact option. With Exact checked, the text must match exactly. The Near option controls whether dBASE tries to find a record that is a near match when it can't find a perfect match for your query. Unless your guru tells you otherwise, leave all the other options alone.

You have several options you can change in the Data Entry category. First, it's just fun to change the sound of the bell. It doesn't fix anything, but it is fun. The other options are a bit more serious. If checked, the Confirm option requires that you press Enter to leave a field after entering data. Normally, dBASE moves you to the next field when you have entered the maximum number of characters in a field. For example, if a field can only hold a two-letter state abbreviation, with Confirm cleared, you are moved to the next field immediately after typing the second character. With Confirm checked, you have to press Enter to move on. A check next to Escape means that you can use the Esc key to stop a program within dBASE. With Escape cleared, you have to wait until the program finishes. The Typeahead value controls how many characters dBASE tries to store if you are typing faster than your computer can record the information. Unfortunately, increasing this value does not work on all computers. Finally, the CUA Enter option controls whether the Enter key moves you between controls on a form (unchecked) or between records (checked).

The Files category contains two boxes in the upper-left corner that can be used to tell dBASE where to check for files — the Search Path and the Current Directory. You can include more than one location in the Search Path by separating the entries with spaces, commas, or semicolons. (I prefer commas myself.) The directory listed for the Current Directory is always checked by the Navigator; those listed in the Search Path are only checked if you have used Properties⇨Navigator to instruct dBASE to Use Supplement Search Path. Note that you don't need to make changes to this information with this dialog box; both the current directory or the search path can also be set from within the Navigator.

Along the bottom of the Files category are two very important sections (plus a catch-all Other group). The Edit Records and Add Records sections are used to select which view is used when you select the Catalog⇨Edit Records and Catalog⇨Add Record commands (or the corresponding Navigator or Table menu commands). You can choose among all three views (Browse, Form, and Columnar) for editing records and between the Columnar Layout and Form Layout for adding records.

The only thing you may want to change in the Application category is the position of the SpeedBar. In my opinion, you shouldn't need to bother with anything in the Programming category.

More stuff

The Sessions option in the Files category controls how distinct the environment is for each table or query. (It's at the bottom in the Other group.) With it checked, you can make changes to a session's environment, which does not change the behavior of other sessions. In other words, with Sessions checked, the settings in the Desktop Properties dialog box are kept separately for each table for features such as the items in the Data Entry category.

Properties⇨Form Designer

Gives you some control over the design of the Form Designer. You can control the way the grid works as well as whether the Form Expert starts automatically for a new form and whether you return to using the pointer after drawing a control.

Just the facts

Most of the options on the Form Designer Properties dialog box are very easy to understand. With names like Show Ruler and Show Grid, you get the idea pretty quickly that inserting a check displays the item within the Form Designer and clearing the option hides the item.

Of course, you do need to know what the grid is to understand most of the choices. The grid is the set of dots that control the placement of controls. With Snap To Grid active (checked), you can only move the edge of a control to a position on the grid. When you are creating new controls and Snap To Grid is checked, each of the control's edges must line up with a dot in the grid.

You use the choices in the Grid Settings section to control the spacing of the dots. If you want to set your own spacing (rather than using the Fine, Medium, or Coarse settings), select Custom and enter spacing values in the boxes for X Grid (spacing across the screen) and Y Grid (spacing up and down the screen). Most people prefer to work with a square grid where the X Grid and Y Grid values are the same, but you're not restricted to this approach.

You should usually leave the Control Palette Draw Mode section set to Bitmap and Text (which gives you somewhat greater flexibility and better quality). As for the two options at the bottom of the dialog box, most of the time you will want to use the pointer cursor immediately after drawing a control, but if you'd rather have the control tool remain selected, clear the Revert to Pointer option. Finally, if you don't like using the Form Expert when you create a new form, clear the Invoke for New Forms option. With it cleared, you start with a blank form whenever you create a new form.

Properties⇨Navigator

Controls the appearance of the various views available within the Navigator. You can set the spacing between the icons and the spacing between the lines in the list when viewing the item details.

Just the facts

From the Navigator, select Properties⇨Navigator to display the Navigator Properties dialog box. In each icon view section (for Large Icons and for Small Icons), you can set both the vertical and horizontal spacing between items (using the X Spacing and Y Spacing boxes). Because the Details view is a list, you can only control the spacing between the lines on the list (the Y Spacing). Select the Reset button for any of the views to use the spacing recommended by the designers of dBASE.

At the bottom of the dialog box is an option called Use Supplemental Search Path. If you check this option *and* have one directory or more listed for the Search Path in the File category under Properties⇨Desktop, dBASE returns any items it can locate in the directories on that list in addition to the current directory. You can also change both the Current Directory and the Search Path directly in the Navigator window.

More stuff

To change the view within the current catalog, use View⇨Large Icons, View⇨Small Icons, or View⇨Details. Use the File category under Properties⇨Desktop to set the supplemental search path.

Properties⇨Query Designer

Determines whether complex indexes are displayed on the Query Designer screen and, therefore, whether they can be used within queries.

Just the facts

Talk about your simple dialog boxes — this has got to be one of the easiest to use. Select Properties⇨Query Designer and you get the Query Designer Properties dialog box, which has only one item: Display Complex Indexes. If the option is checked, any complex indexes in the tables are shown on the Query Designer screen. If it's cleared, the complex indexes aren't shown.

More stuff

Of course, it helps if you know what a complex index actually is. When you create a database table, you can create indexes for fields within the table. Creating an index for a field reduces the time it takes to find matching records for queries using those fields. You can also create complex indexes that combine information from more than one field and therefore improve the performance of queries using that combination of fields.

Displaying the complex indexes makes it easier to create a query that takes advantage of those indexed fields. In an ideal world, a query that uses all of the fields in a complex index, and only those fields, would be significantly faster than one that uses almost all the fields in the complex index or one that uses any additional fields. Unfortunately, this isn't an ideal world, but you usually see some improvement in speed.

To create a complex index, use Table⇨Table Utilities⇨Manage Indexes (where the steps are described), or either Query⇨Manage Indexes or Structure⇨Manage Indexes (which work the same).

Properties⇨Selected Catalog Item

Displays the file and catalog information for the selected item. For most items, you can also change the item's description.

For keyboard krazies

Just the facts

Select the item and then select Properties⇨Selected Catalog Item or press Alt+Enter. For most items, the only thing you can do other than look at the information is change the description. But, then again, what else would you want to do?

More stuff

The SpeedMenu (which you reach by selecting the item and clicking the right mouse button) lists a command specific to the type of item selected (such as Query Properties or Label Properties). But the dialog boxes for these commands are all the same as what you find under Properties⇨Selected Catalog Item.

You can display much of the same information within your catalog by selecting View⇨Details.

Properties⇨Selected File Item

Displays the file information for the selected item. Unlike Catalog⇨Selected Catalog Item, there is no file description, and you cannot change any of the information.

For keyboard krazies

Just the facts

Select the item you'd like to know more about and then select Properties⇨Selected File Item. Look at the information and then select OK to close the dialog box.

More stuff

To see most of the same information while working in the Navigator, select View⇨Details.

Properties⇨Table Records Window

Controls the data entry for fields, the format of the window, and not only which records you can see in the table but what you can do with the records as well.

Just the facts

The simplest category within the Table Records Properties dialog box (which is what you get when you select Properties⇨Table Records Window) is the one for the Window settings (shown in the following figure). The absolute simplest setting is for the Title of the window that contains the table: just enter the text you want displayed in the title bar. You can also control whether the lines between records and fields are displayed. (Horizontal Grid controls the lines between records, and Vertical Grid controls the lines between fields.) The Toggle Layout option determines whether you can use commands on the View menu (such as View⇨Browse Layout or View⇨Field Contents) to change the view of your data. A check next to any of these options means that the feature is available (the lines are showing, or you can toggle the layout).

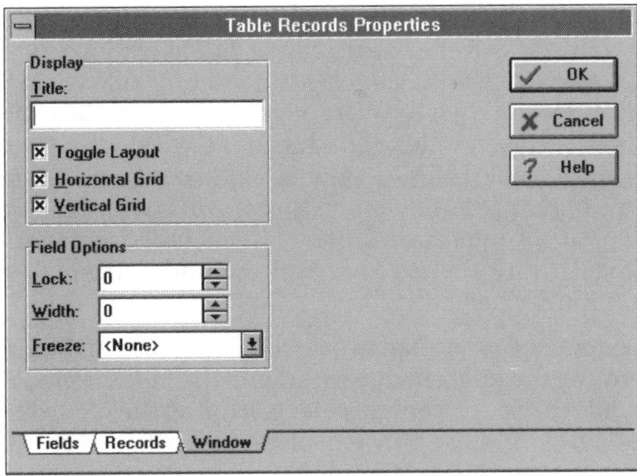

You can use the other settings in the Window category to control some aspects of data entry and display. Use the Lock option to control how many fields are always displayed at the left side of the browse display. The number you enter represents how many fields will stay in position when you scroll through the records from left to right. For example, a value of two means that the first and second fields are always displayed no matter what other fields are showing. Use the Width option to set the standard width for character fields. You can override this setting for individual fields by using the Properties button in the Fields category as described below. Use the Freeze option to limit data entry to only the selected field.

Two distinct groups of features are available within the Records category. In the upper-left corner are the Editing Options. The four entries in this section control what actions can be performed within the table. If an entry is checked, then that action can be performed. If it is cleared, then the command associated with that action won't even be available. The four choices are Append (associated with Table⇨Add Records), Edit (which controls whether you can make changes to the contents of the fields), Delete (Table⇨Table Utilities⇨Delete Records or Table⇨Delete Selected Record), and Follow Index (which controls what happens when you edit the contents of the field used to index the records). If Follow Index is cleared, when you change the index value, the record is moved to its new location, but your position within the table does not change. With it checked, your position moves to follow the record.

The remainder of the dialog box is used to control which items are displayed. You can use the Index Range section to limit the display to records with values in the primary index field between the Low Key and High Key. Of course, you need to know what field is the primary index and a bit about working with indexes (see Table⇨Table Utilities⇨Manage Indexes for more info). The Exclude option determines whether records with values equal to the two values entered as the keys are included and therefore displayed (the option is cleared) or excluded and not displayed (the option is checked).

The Scope section is used to select records within the group selected by the Index Range settings. If the Index Range boxes are left blank, the Scope section selects from all the records in the table. You can choose between displaying All the records, the Rest of the records (starting with the current record), a certain number of records following the current one (the Next few), or a specific Record (by record number). For further control over which records are displayed, use a *scope expression*. A scope expression is similar to a query condition except that you have to include the actual field name in the expression. Use a For scope expression to select which records to print. Use a While scope expression to continue displaying the next records until the expression is no longer true. You can combine a For scope expression with the All, Next, or Rest options. For example, you can display only the next ten records where the State field contains the value *WA* by putting **State="WA"** in the For box and **10** in the Next box. In general, you don't combine While with any other option. You can use the Expression Builder to help you create a scope expression. (The Next and Record options are not available when working in Browse Layout.)

Finally, the settings in the Fields category control the process of entering data into the fields. This is probably the most important dialog box in all of dBASE. The Selected Fields list selects which fields are to be displayed in the table, and the Available Fields list contains the records in the table that are not to be displayed. You can use the buttons between the two lists to move fields between them. The double arrowheads (<< and >>) move the entire list in the direction indicated. The single arrowheads (< and >) move only the selected field.

Click the Add Calculated Field button to open a simple dialog box where you can name a new calculated field and create the expression for calculating the values for the field. If you click the little wrench icon, you can use the Expression Builder to create the expression (see Edit⇨Build Expression). You can select a calculated field and select the Calculated button to change the expression used for the calculation.

The most powerful feature is the Properties button, which is near the bottom of the dialog box. When you select a field and then click the Properties button, you get the dialog box shown here.

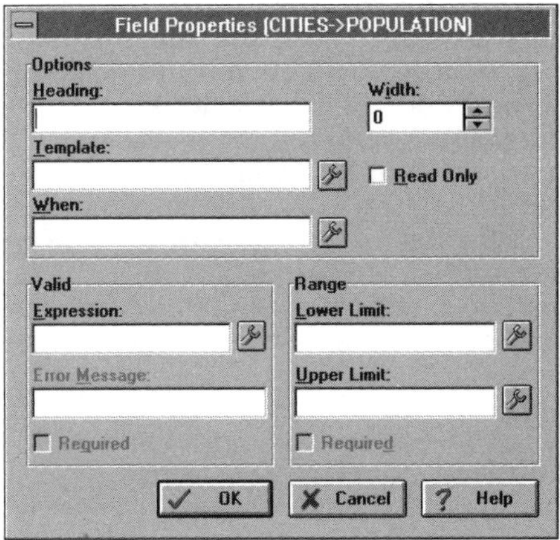

One of the easiest things you can do is create a heading for the field. The advantage to using a heading instead of the field name is that a heading can contain spaces and lowercase letters. For example, you can use *Amount Paid* rather than AMT_PAID. You may need to adjust the Width of the field to display the whole heading (or to get rid of extra space).

The Read Only option should only be checked if you want to create a field that cannot be edited. Calculated fields are automatically set for Read Only. Use the When box to create an expression that must be true before the field can be edited. Usually, your expression depends on a value in another field. For example, you may only allow the ZIP_CODE field to be edited when the COUNTRY field contains the value *USA*.

You can also use a template to control how the field's contents are displayed. Click the button at the left of the box (the button has a little wrench on it) to open the Choose Template dialog box. Within the dialog box are three tabs for the three categories of template codes: Character, Numeric, and Date. Select the appropriate category and then choose a combination of codes from the list. You can use any combination of formatting codes (which control how the contents of the field are displayed) or data entry codes (which limit what can be entered into the field). When you select a code, the description of what it does is displayed in the middle of the dialog box. Double-click the code to add it to the Template box. Click OK to return the Field Properties and to use the codes listed in the Template box.

The remaining sections are used to control what values can be entered into the field. You can use the Range section to put an Upper Limit, Lower Limit, or both on the values that are acceptable within the field. You can also create an Expression in the Valid section that must be true for the value to be accepted. When you create a Valid Expression, you should use the current field within the expression. For example, you may have an expression for the AMT_RECEIVED field that says **AMT_RECEIVED >= AMT_DUE**. You can use the button at the right of the field to open the Expression Builder and create the expression. The text in the Error Message box will be displayed if someone tries to enter a value that makes the Expression false. You can use either or both of these methods to restrict values for the field. Use the associated Required option to require that an acceptable value be entered into the field before the user can move to another field.

More stuff

Whereas you use Properties⇨Table Records Window to determine whether you can delete records in the table, you use the Table category within Properties⇨Desktop to control whether records marked for deletion are displayed. The format for some of the templates is set with the Country category of Properties⇨Desktop. Use of the For and While scope expressions is covered in the Glossary.

Properties⇨Table Structure Window

Determines whether the window that lists the field definitions has lines showing between the rows and columns.

Just the facts

One of the simpler dialog boxes in dBASE, the Table Structure Properties dialog box (which is what you get when you select Properties⇨Table Structure Window while viewing the structure of a table) has only two settings: Horizontal Grid Lines and Vertical Grid Lines. A check next to an option means that those lines will be displayed. If the option is cleared, no lines appear in that direction. Horizontal lines separate the rows for each field, and vertical lines separate the columns of information.

More stuff

For one of the most complex dialog boxes, see Properties⇨Table Records Window, which controls how the fields in the table are displayed and what values are acceptable within each field.

Properties⇨Text Editor

Controls the behavior of the standard dBASE Text Editor.

Just the facts

The feature you're most likely to want to change is Word Wrap, which controls whether the lines are adjusted to fit in the window or whether each line is displayed the same way as you enter it. With Word Wrap turned off (no check next to it), your lines can continue beyond the right edge of the window. Put a check next to Word Wrap to have the Text Editor work more like a word processor. With Word Wrap selected, you can use the Right Margin box to indicate the number of characters that can fit on a single line (rather than using the width of the window). Use the value of zero to allow as many characters as will fit within the window. You can use the button at the right edge of the Font box to select a font to be used within the Text Editor window. For most people, that's all there is of interest in this dialog box.

If you happen to be writing a program, you won't want to put a check next to Word Wrap, and you may care about the other settings. For example, you can indent one line and automatically have the following lines start at the same indentation. If that's what you want, put a check next to Auto Indent and specify the number of characters to move when you press the Tab key in the Spacing box. The Auto Colors feature causes special programming elements to appear in different colors. If you're not programming, then all Auto Colors does is make your text more colorful. If you are programming, it makes it easier to identify the different elements of your program.

More stuff

Use Shift+Tab to move back to the start of the previous indentation when using the Auto Indent feature.

This same dialog box is used for setting the characteristics of the Program Editor and Procedure Editor, although the settings for each are stored separately.

Query⇨Add Conditions

Provides another way of creating a condition within a query. Instead of adding an expression into a table, you can create an entire expression (including the field names) in the Conditions area. This option is most useful if you want to write a condition that relies on a calculation involving two or more fields.

Just the facts

Well, it's actually quite a simple command to use. Select Query⇨Add Conditions, and the Conditions area appears at the bottom of your query. Now, to use the Conditions area effectively requires a bit more work. In general, you should put any queries that require only a single field into the tables in the upper portion of your query. Reserve the Conditions area for those queries that require more than one field. When you work in the Conditions area, you need to include the field names as well as the other query conditions.

For example, you may want to display only those records where the amount ordered is greater than $1000. If your tables include a field for the number ordered (QUANTITY) and another for PRICE, you have the information you need, but no place to put it. You don't have a condition for either QUANTITY or PRICE, but instead one that involves both fields. One way to get around this would be to create a calculated field for something like TOTAL_COST (equal to QUANTITY * PRICE), but that would add an extra field to your table and take up a great deal of room. Even worse, the two fields may be in different tables. Fortunately, there's an easier way: use the Conditions area. After you've added the Conditions area, enter your query — in this case, something like **QUANTITY * PRICE > 1000**. You've now created a condition in your query that uses two separate fields.

More stuff

Use AND and OR conditions to create more complex rules. As with fields in the Query Designer, use the down-arrow to get a new line for an OR condition and put each expression on its own line. For an AND condition, put the information on the same line, with a comma separating each pair of expressions.

In reality, you can also add a calculated field to your query rather than to one of your tables. This feature is useful when you want to display the results of the calculation as part of the query results. When you use the Conditions area, you cannot display the formula results as part of the query results.

For more on creating a query using the fields in the Query Designer, see Catalog⇨New Query. To get rid of the Conditions area, use Query⇨Remove Conditions. To add a calculated field to your query but not to one of your tables, use Query⇨Create Calculated Field.

Query⇨Add Table

Adds a new table to the Query Designer. You need to have a table displayed within the Query Designer to use any of that table's fields as part of a condition or to display any of its fields in the query result.

For keyboard krazies

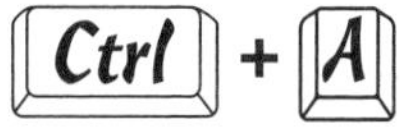

For mouse maniacs

Click this button to open a dialog box where you can select a table to add to the current query.

Just the facts

Select Query⇨Add Table, and you get a list of all the database tables that dBASE can locate. Simply click the table that you want and then click the OK button (or double-click the table). That's it. The table you selected is now on the Query Designer screen. To add another table, you have to select Query⇨Add Table again.

More stuff

To find out what to do with a table once it's in the Query Designer, see Catalog⇨New Query.

Query⇨Copy Results to New Table

Takes the query results and uses them as the contents for a new table. Sometimes this is the most useful command in the world, and other times it can cause significant problems.

Just the facts

Before you use this command, you need to have created your query with all of its conditions. The Query⇨Copy Results to New Table command takes the query results and, from them, creates a new table. Once you've created the new table, it is independent of anything you do in the original table.

To create a table of query results, select Query⇨Copy Results to New Table, which brings up the Save Table dialog box asking you to save the new table. The advantage to creating a new table with the copied results is that you can use the new table as its own database, which is useful when you need to send part, but not all, of your database to someone else or when you need to do a lot of work with the same group of records.

More stuff

The disadvantage to creating new tables from your query results is that if you use this command too often, you end with up too many tables on your computer. Not only do all these tables take up memory, but, in most cases, only the original table is updated with new information, meaning that the records in all the newly created tables quickly become out of date.

Query⇨Create Calculated Field

Adds the Calculated area (if it's not already displayed) and creates a new calculated field. You must provide both a field name and an expression for calculating the field.

Just the facts

Select Query⇨Create Calculated Field and you find yourself in the Calculated area. The field name is the abbreviation *CALC* followed by a number. The first thing you should do is replace this name with something a bit more meaningful. Just select the old name and type the new name.

Now you need to enter the expression for calculating the values for the fields. To do that, move to the second line (which starts with an equal sign) and enter the expression. This is one of those times when the Expression Builder might come in handy, but it's not available. You have to create the expression using the fields in the tables that are displayed in the Query Designer, the math operators (+, -, and so on), and any functions you need.

Once you've entered the expression, you're done. You can now use the calculated field just like any other field in the Query Designer. You can give it a condition, display it in the results, or perform some combination of these actions.

More stuff

For more information on using a field in a query, see Catalog⇨New Query. To create a condition that uses more than one field without creating a new calculated field, use Query⇨Add Conditions. To add a calculated field to a table, use the Fields category in Properties⇨Table Records Window.

Query⇨Delete Selected Calculated Field

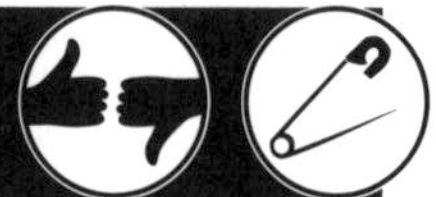

Removes the selected field from the Calculated area. Although it can be annoying to accidentally remove a calculated field, it isn't too bad because you can always re-create it.

Just the facts

Make sure that you are in the right field (in other words, the one you want to get rid of) and then select Query⇨Delete Selected Calculated Field. Faster than you can say the name of the command, the field is removed. If it's the only calculated field in the Calculated area, the entire Calculated area is removed.

More stuff

To add a calculated field to the Query Designer, use Query⇨Create Calculated Field.

Query⇨Manage Indexes

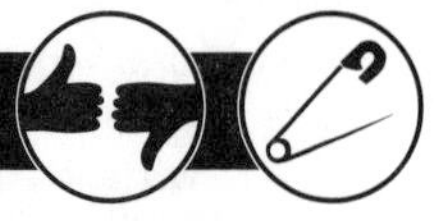

Lets you create, modify, or delete indexes for the tables being displayed. This is the same command as Table⇨Table Utilities⇨Manage Indexes, and that's where you are going to have to look for an explanation.

Query⇨Modify Relation

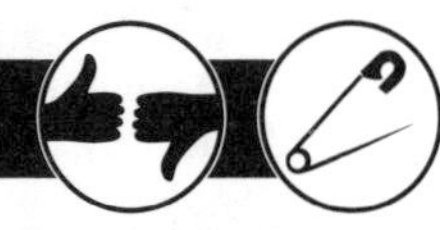

Gives you the opportunity to make changes to the relationship between the selected table and its parent. The selected table must be one that is pointed to by a relationship arrow (and indented under its parent). The parent table is the one that is at the other end of the arrow. The relationship arrows appear at the left side of the Query Designer.

Just the facts

You have to be in the child table of the relationship, which means that the table you're in must be indented, and the relationship you're modifying must be the one represented by the arrow from the table above the current one. Clearly, I need a picture to explain this.

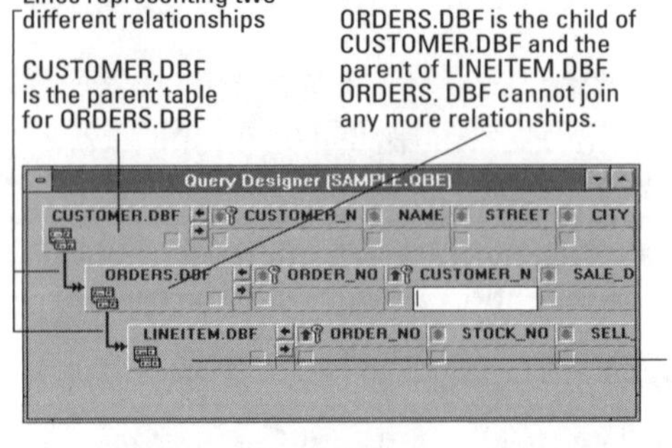

Once you've figured out where you need to be to modify the desired relationship, the rest of the procedure is almost exactly the same as setting up the relationship to begin with. The only difference is that you cannot change the tables involved in the relationship.

More stuff

To find out about the dialog box used to set up or modify a relationship, see Query⇨Set Relation.

Query⇨Remove Conditions

Removes the Conditions area from your Query Designer screen. This command doesn't change any conditions listed within the fields for the tables on the Query Designer screen.

Just the facts

All you need to do is select Query⇨Remove Conditions; the Conditions area disappears.

More stuff

To find out what the Conditions area is for and how it got on your screen in the first place, see Query⇨Add Conditions.

Query⇨Remove Relation

Removes the relationship between the current table and its parent. The parent is the table that appears above the current table (follow the arrow back to find the parent table).

For mouse maniacs

Click the button to break up a happy home — it removes the relationship between the current table and its parent.

Just the facts

Why is it always so much easier to destroy things than to create them? I mean, you spend hours making sure that the relationship is exactly what you want, but when you select Query⇨Remove Relation, it disappears immediately. Oh, well, the relationship probably wasn't any good for you, anyway.

More stuff

For a picture to help you figure out which relationship you are going to be getting rid of, see Query⇨Modify Relation. To create a relationship, see Query⇨Set Relation. (Sorry, this won't help your personal life.)

Query⇨Remove Selected Table

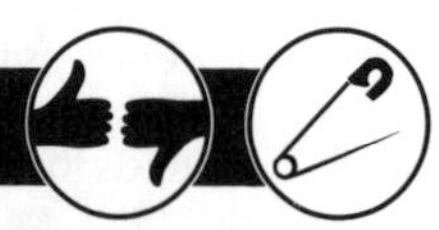

Removes the selected table from the Query Designer screen. Don't worry — the table isn't removed from your disk or from the catalog (if you're using one).

For mouse maniacs

Make sure you're in the table you want to remove and click this button. The table is gone from the Query Designer.

Just the facts

Move to the table you want to remove and then select Query⇨Remove Selected Table. That's pretty much all you can do with this command.

More stuff

To add a table to your query, use Query⇨Add Table.

Query⇨Set Relation

Creates a relationship between two tables. When two tables are related, you can display related records from the two tables in the same query.

For mouse maniacs

Click this button to open the dialog box for creating relationships between tables.

Just the facts

Before you get started, it's important to have some idea of what a relationship between two tables actually means. The key thing is that each of the two tables must have a field that contains the same values and which is used to relate the tables. That field has to exist in both tables and usually has the same name.

Since the terms used to describe these relationships are parent table and child table, I decided to use the example of mothers and children. In dBASE, a child record can only have one parent, but a parent record can be linked to no child records, one child record, or a group of child records. In biology, a child can have only one mother, but a woman can have no children, one child, or children. (Ignore adoption and science fiction for the moment please!)

In this example, you have a MOTHERS table, with detailed information about each mother in the table as well as a unique identifying code for each mother (in the MOM field for that table). In a separate table (called CHILDREN), you may have a list of all the children with their descriptive information and a code indicating the mother of each child (in a field also called MOM). The CHILDREN table doesn't contain any information about the mothers (other than the identifying code in the MOM field), and the MOTHERS table doesn't contain any information about the children.

You create a relationship between the two tables by relating the two MOM fields (one in each table). To keep the two fields separate, you need to use their full names — the table name followed by the field name (MOTHERS⇨MOM and CHILDREN⇨MOM). Once you've defined the relationship, dBASE can then look at a record in the MOTHERS table (with its unique code in the MOTHERS⇨MOM field) and check for any records in the CHILDREN table with the same value in the CHILDREN⇨MOM field. Each record in the CHILDREN table with a matching value in the MOM field is a child of the record in the MOTHERS table. With this link, when dBASE finds a record in the CHILDREN table with the same value, it can display the description of that child along with the related mother.

First, it's easiest if you move to one of the tables that will be used for the relationship. The table you select must be free to join a relationship — a single table can have a maximum of two relationships. To create a relationship, you need to open the Define Relation dialog box (shown here) by selecting Query⇨Set Relation or use the button described in the "For mouse maniacs" section.

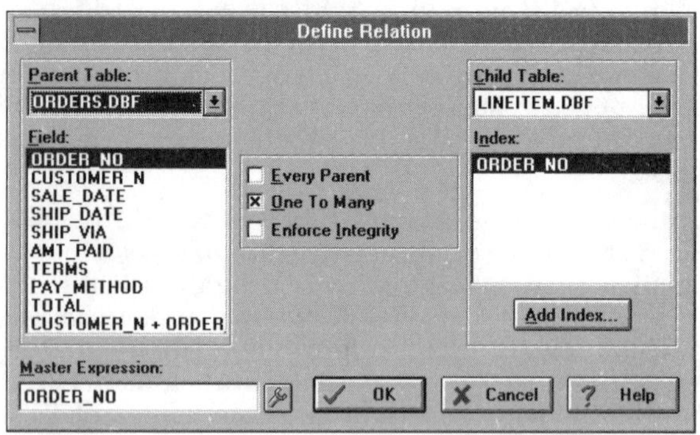

Select the table that is to be the parent from the Parent Table list on the left side. Then select the field that represents the relationship in that table from the list on the left. Select the second table from the Child Table list. Only fields that are indexed appear in the Child Table list on the right; if the field used for the relationship in that table is not displayed, select the Add Index button and create an index for the field you want to use. Once you've created a relationship, the parent field is displayed in the Master Expression box.

You can now refine which records are included in the relationship by using the option buttons in the middle of the dialog box. A check next to Every Parent causes every parent record to be displayed regardless of whether it has a corresponding child record. If the option isn't checked, only those parent records that are related to a child record are displayed. A check next to One To Many causes every child record for a given parent to be displayed. If the One To Many option is cleared, only the first child record is displayed.

The Enforce Integrity option changes the way in which you can edit the data in the two tables. When it is checked, it requires that any child record be related to a parent record. If you delete a parent record, you must delete all child records. If you add a child record, it must have an acceptable value linking it to one of the existing parent records. So to add both a parent record and a child record, you must add the parent record first. The Enforce Integrity option is really more related to the design of your table rather than just getting an answer to your query and is a topic best left to the gurus.

More stuff

The terms *parent* and *child* refer to the direction of the relationship between the two tables. Each record in the parent table must have a unique value for the field used in the relationship. The field used for the relationship in the child table must be indexed. The arrows at the left of the Query Designer screen always point to the child table, and the other end is connected to the parent. A single parent can have many children, one child, or no children. Each child should have a parent, but dBASE only requires this when the Enforce Integrity option is checked.

Another way to open the Define Relation dialog box is by dragging the icon at the left edge of one table to the same area on the table to which you want to relate the first table. When you put your cursor over the left edge, the cursor should change to two small tables connected with an arrow. When you hold down the mouse button, you should see a line extending from your cursor back to the icon. With the mouse button down, drag the line so that it connects the two tables and then release the button. You should be in the Define Relation dialog box.

For information on working with more than one table of data, see Chapter 18 of *dBASE For Windows For Dummies*.

For more on creating indexes, see Table⇨Table Utilities⇨Manage Indexes.

Report⇨Bottom Page

Jumps to the last page in your report (which will be the "bottom page" once you've printed your report and put the pages in the right order).

For keyboard krazies

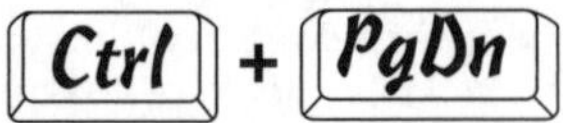

For mouse maniacs

Click here to jump to the last page of the report.

Just the facts

Select Report⇨Bottom Page (or one of its shortcuts) and hang on, as you are immediately transported to the last page in the report.

More stuff

Use the scroll bars to move around on the report page.

The other commands on the Record menu (Record⇨Next Page, Record⇨Previous Page, and Record⇨Top Page) also move you through the report.

Report⇨Next Page

Moves you forward a single page within the current report.

For keyboard krazies

For mouse maniacs

Click this button to move to the next page of the report.

Just the facts

Selecting Report⇨Next Page is the same as turning a page in a printed report. You move forward a single page through the document.

More stuff

You need to use the scroll bars to move around on the report page.

Record⇨Bottom Page, Record⇨Previous Page, and Record⇨Top Page also move you through the report.

Report⇨Previous Page

Goes back one page in the current report.

For keyboard krazies

For mouse maniacs

Click this button to go to the previous page of the report.

Just the facts

This is the reverse command, useful when you suddenly realize that you don't remember what you just read. Select Report⇨Previous Page and you go back a single page.

More stuff

If you want to move around on the current page of the report, you need to use the scroll bars.

Use Record⇨Bottom Page and Record⇨Top Page to jump to the beginning or end of your report. Use Record⇨Next Page to move a single page forward.

Report⇨Top Page

Jumps to the start of the report without passing Go and without collecting $200.

For keyboard krazies

Ctrl + PgUp

For mouse maniacs

Click here for the express elevator to the first page of the report.

Just the facts

When you want to start over, just select Report⇨Top Page and you find yourself at the beginning of the report.

More stuff

The scroll bars can be used to move around on the report page.

Record⇨Bottom Page jumps you to the last page in the report. Record⇨Next Page and Record⇨Previous Page move you at a more leisurely pace.

Structure⇨Add Field

Adds a new field at the bottom of the table.

For keyboard krazies

Ctrl + A

For mouse maniacs

Click this button to add a blank field definition at the end of the structure.

Just the facts

It doesn't matter where you are when you select Structure⇨Add Field; the new field is added at the end of the structure. Once you've added the field, you need to fill in the information describing the field.

More stuff

Another way to get a new definition at the end of your table is by going to the last field definition and pressing Enter or Tab until a new row is created.

For more on defining the structure of a field, see Catalog⇨New Table. For information about rearranging the fields within a table, see Structure⇨Insert Field.

Structure⇨Delete Selected Field

Removes the selected field from the table's structures. Be careful, because if your table already has records, any information contained in the field is also removed.

For keyboard krazies

For mouse maniacs

Make sure that you are on the field you want to get rid of before selecting this button.

Just the facts

Move to the field you want to get rid of and select Structure⇨Delete Selected Field. Be warned that there isn't any warning — the field just disappears.

More stuff

Only when you go to save the table's new structure are you warned that deleting or changing a field can result in losing some or all of your data. At that point, it's too late, so remember to be careful when you delete a record.

If you want to rearrange the fields in your table, see Structure⇨Insert Field.

Structure⇨Go to Field Number

Gives you a menu command for moving between field definitions in the table's structures.

For keyboard krazies

Just the facts

When you select Structure⇨Go to Field Number, you get a dialog box where you just need to type the number of the proper field and press Enter. Then you find yourself at that field.

More stuff

Usually, using the scroll bars is the easiest way to move through the definitions; then just click the field you want to work with. I mean, really, who remembers the numbers for particular fields?

Structure⇨Insert Field

Adds a new field definition before the current field. This command is useful if you want to keep the field definitions in some sort of logical order.

For keyboard krazies

For mouse maniacs

Click this button to add a field definition above the current row.

Just the facts

Move to the field definition that will follow the one you're going to insert and select Structure⇨Insert Field. All the fields below and including the current one are moved down one line, and you get a new, blank definition on the row where you were working. You can now complete the field definition for your new field.

More stuff

If you want to move a field definition, just place your cursor over the field number (at the far left) and wait for the little grasping hand. Once it appears, hold down the mouse button and drag the field to its new location. When you are displaying a table, you can also rearrange the order of the columns using the same technique: put the cursor over the field name (or heading) and drag the column to the new location. The order of the field definitions is independent of the order of the columns when displaying the table.

For instructions about what to do with your field definition after you create it, see Catalog⇨New Table.

Structure⇨Manage Indexes

Creates, modifies, or deletes indexes for the current table. This is the same command as Table⇨Table Utilities⇨Manage Indexes, which is where you need to look for more of an explanation.

Table⇨Add Records

Creates a blank record at the end of the table for your data entry pleasure.

For keyboard krazies

For mouse maniacs

Click this button and you're moved to the bottom of the table, where you'll find a new blank record.

Just the facts

Select Table⇨Add Records to add new records at the end of the table. Immediately after selecting the command, you find yourself at the end of the table in a new, blank record. Just start filling it in. When you get to the end of the record, you can press Tab or Enter to get another new record.

More stuff

Any new entries are saved for each field in the record as you move to the next field. You can move to another field by pressing Tab or Enter or by clicking somewhere else.

You can open a table and immediately start adding records by using Catalog⇨Add Records (or Navigator⇨Add Records, if you don't use catalogs).

Table⇨Blank Selected Record

Clears out all the information in the selected record so that you can try again. Sometimes this method is easier than deleting a record and creating a new one.

Just the facts

Make sure that you're in the record you want to clear out and then select Table⇨Blank Selected Record. Whoosh! All of that old data is gone, and you can start over with new information.

More stuff

To just add new information, use Table⇨Add Records.

Table⇨Bottom Record

Jumps to the end of the current table.

For keyboard krazies

For mouse maniacs

Click this button to go to the last record in the table.

Just the facts

Select Table⇨Bottom Record and you find yourself in the last record in your table.

More stuff

Table⇨Next Record moves you down one record, and Table⇨Next Page moves you down one screen-full of records. You can use Table⇨Previous Record, Table⇨Previous Page, and Table⇨Top Record to move back toward the start of the table. Table⇨Go to Record Number moves you to a specific record.

Table⇨Create Query

Creates a brand new query in the Query Designer. This command is the same as selecting File⇨New⇨Query, but you'll find the steps described under Catalog⇨New Query.

Table⇨Delete Selected Record

Marks the selected record for deletion. To actually remove the record, you need to use Table⇨Table Utilities⇨Pack Records. Whether the records that are marked for deletion are displayed is controlled by the Deleted option in the Table category under Properties⇨Desktop.

For keyboard krazies

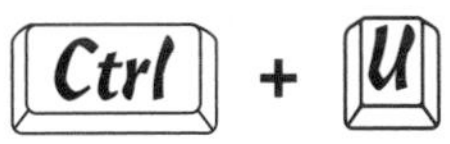

Just the facts

When you select Table⇨Delete Selected Record (or press Ctrl+U), the current record is marked for deletion. The setting for the Deleted option in the Table category of the Desktop Properties is relevant here: if Deleted is checked, a deleted record disappears from the table even though it is still in the file; if Deleted is cleared, an X appears in the Del column to indicate that the record you just deleted is marked for deletion. No matter which way Deleted is set, the "deleted" record is only *marked* for deletion. To actually remove it from the file, you need to use Table⇨Table Utilities⇨Pack Records.

More stuff

You can change whether the records marked for deletion are displayed while you're working with a table by pressing Alt, P, D, T, Enter — that is, Properties⇨Desktop, Deleted, OK.

If you are displaying the records marked for deletion, you can also mark a record by putting a mark in the Del column (at the left, next to the record number). Records that have a red X are marked for deletion; those without are not.

To mark a group of records for deletion, use Table⇨Table Utilities⇨Delete Records. To actually remove records marked for deletion, use Table⇨Table Utilities⇨Pack Records. To delete records in a single step, use Table⇨Table Utilities⇨Zap Records. If you clear Deleted in the Table category under Desktop Properties, you can use Table⇨Recall Selected Record to recall the current record (assuming that it's marked for deletion) or Table⇨Table Utilities⇨Recall Records to recall a group of marked records.

Table⇨Find Records

Searches for a record or group of records based on the rules you create. You can look for a particular word or part of a phrase in any single field in your table.

For keyboard krazies

For mouse maniacs

Click this button to open the dialog box that you use to find any records with matching text.

Just the facts

Table⇨Find Records is probably located at the top of the menu because it is one of the most useful and most used commands. Often, you need to find something in your database, but it doesn't seem worth the trouble of designing a query. That's when you can use Table⇨Find Records to locate what you are looking for. When you first select Table⇨Find Records, you get a dialog box like the one shown here.

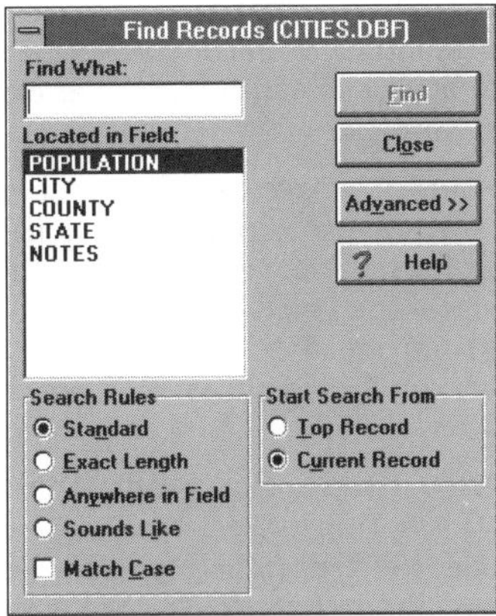

The most important parts of the dialog box are the Find What box and the Located in Field list in the upper-left area. Put what you're looking for in the Find What box. Generally, a search consists of the word or phrase that you're trying to find, although you can use part of a word or an expression. (For more on searching for expressions, see the first tip under More stuff.) You then need to select which field to search in the Located in Field list. These two items are actually all you need to search for something, but a number of other options exist to make your search more precise and to control the results.

To start a search, simply click the Find button. One thing you should be aware of is that the Find Records dialog box stays open as you move through the records. To see the records hidden by the Find Records dialog box, either move the box (by dragging the title bar where it says Find Records) or select the Close button.

In the lower-left of the dialog box are the Search Rules options for setting how dBASE looks for the text you put into the Find What box. You can choose between Standard (the text must start the field, but there can be additional text), Exact Match (the text must be the only thing in the field), Anywhere in Field (the text can be anywhere in the field), and Sounds Like (dBASE tries to find text anywhere in the field that is similar to what you put in the Find What box). These options are listed in order of speed, with Standard being the fastest type of search and Sounds Like the slowest. Note that with numeric and date fields, dBASE always looks for an Exact Match, so these options aren't available.

At the end of the group is a check box, Match Case, which can be used with any of the first three Search Rules (but not with Sounds Like). When there is a check next to Match Case, the text in the field must match the text in the Find What box exactly in terms of upper- and lowercase letters. In other words, with Match Case checked, *dBASE* would only match *dBASE*, not *dBase*, *DBASE,* or *dbase*. With Match Case cleared, any of the four styles of capitalization would match any of the others.

When you select the Find button, you go to the first record that matches the information you have provided. But which is the *first* record depends on where you start, so you have to decide between starting the search at the Top Record or at the Current Record. If you are moving from one match to another, always use Current Record; otherwise, you'll keep finding the same record at the start of the file.

Although you can use the Advanced button to open the Scope section of the dialog box, this option makes more sense when working with Table⇨Replace Records (which uses the same dialog box) and is discussed under that topic rather than here.

More stuff

In addition to simply searching for words or values in a single field, you can search by comparing the value in the selected field to values in other fields for the same record. This type of search uses an expression created with other fields and then, for each record, compares the expression's value with the contents of the current field. For example, you may want to locate someone who has the same phone number listed under both HOME_PHONE and WORK_PHONE. Select HOME_PHONE in the Located in Field list and enter **(WORK_PHONE)** in the Find What box. For each record, this expression uses the value from WORK_PHONE as the Find What text and then checks to see if it matches the value in the current field, HOME_PHONE. The parentheses tell dBASE that you are using an expression that needs to be calculated for each record. You can perform any type of calculation within the expression.

If you want to search the first field in the Located in Field list, be sure to click it even though it looks as though it's already selected when you open the dialog box. The other options in the dialog box aren't updated for the field until you actually select the field.

For more about tracking down information in your database, see Chapter 11 in *dBASE For Windows For Dummies*.

Use Table⇨Replace Records to find all matches to your text and change them into something else. If you're searching a memo field, Table⇨Find Records locates a field that contains the text. You may need to open the memo field itself and use Edit⇨Search⇨Find Text to find the precise location.

Table⇨Go to Record Number

Jumps you to the record you request.

For keyboard krazies

Just the facts

After you select Table⇨Go to Record Number, you need to provide a record number in the dialog box. Then, when you press Enter, you jump right to that record.

More stuff

Use Table⇨Next Record, Table⇨Bottom Record, and Table⇨Next Page to move forward through your table. You can use Table⇨Previous Record, Table⇨Top Record, and Table⇨Previous Page to move back toward the start of the table.

Table⇨Lock Selected Record

Locks the record so that no one else in your multiuser environment (which means that other people are using the same table at the same time) can make changes to that record.

For keyboard krazies

Just the facts

Move to the record you want to lock and select Table⇨Lock Selected Record. Now, only you can make changes to that record. Anyone else trying to change the record will get a dialog box saying that the record is locked. Other people can still use information from the record, but they can't *change* that information.

More stuff

Well, if you can lock something, you should be able to unlock it. Sure enough, when you're in a locked record, the command changes to Table⇨Unlock Selected Record.

Table⇨Next Page

Jumps to the next screen of records (with one overlapping record still on-screen).

For keyboard krazies

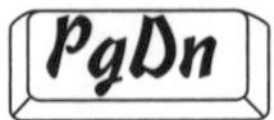

For mouse maniacs

Click this button to display the next screen of records.

Just the facts

Select Table⇨Next Page and you move to the next screen of records. What used to be the last record showing on-screen is now at the top.

More stuff

Table⇨Previous Page jumps you back one full screen. You can also use Table⇨Previous Record or Table⇨Top Record to move toward the start of the table, and Table⇨Bottom Record or Table⇨Next Record to move toward the end of the table. Use Table⇨Go to Record Number to move to a specific record.

Table⇨Next Record

Moves down a single record. This command is useful when you need to carefully read through your records or when you're working with the Form view.

For keyboard krazies

For mouse maniacs

Click on this button to move down a record.

Just the facts

Select Table⇨Next Record to move to the next record, which is the one *below* the record you're working with in Browse view.

More stuff

Table⇨Previous Record backs you up a single record. Table⇨Top Record jumps to the start of the table, and Table⇨Bottom Record jumps to the end. Table⇨Next Page moves you down one screen-full of records, and Table⇨Previous Page moves you back toward the start of the table. Table⇨Go to Record Number jumps to a specific record.

Table⇨Previous Page

Moves back toward the start of the file and displays a full screen of records.

For keyboard krazies

For mouse maniacs

Clicking this button displays the previous screen of records.

Just the facts

Select Table⇨Previous Page and you can see the full screen of records immediately before the ones you were just working with. The record that was at the top of the screen is now at the bottom.

More stuff

To move forward a screen-full of records, use Table⇨Next Page. To jump to the start of the table, use Table⇨Top Record; to jump to the end, use Table⇨Bottom Record. You can use Table⇨Next Record to move down one record and Table⇨Previous Record to move back one record. Table⇨Go to Record Number moves you to a specific record.

Table⇨Previous Record

Moves you a single record back toward the start of the file. This command is useful if you need to carefully move through your records or if you're working in Form view.

For keyboard krazies

For mouse maniacs

Click this button to move up one record in your table.

Just the facts

Select Table⇨Previous Record to view the record immediately before the one you're working with.

More stuff

Use Table⇨Next Record to move down one record. Even more useful are Table⇨Next Page and Table⇨Previous Page, which move you one screen-full of records down and up, respectively. You can use Table⇨Bottom Record or Table⇨Top Record when you want to jump to the end or start of the table. Finally, Table⇨Go to Record Number moves you to a specific record.

Table⇨Recall Selected Record

Recalls a record that is marked for deletion, which means that the record is no longer marked. You can only use this command if you are displaying deleted records (by clearing the Deleted option in the Table category under Properties⇨Desktop).

For keyboard krazies

Just the facts

To use this command, you must be able to view the records that are marked for deletion. To do that, clear the Deleted option in the Table category on the Desktop Properties dialog box (Properties⇨Desktop). You can change the setting of this option at any time.

When you move to a record marked for deletion, you can select Table⇨Recall Selected Record (which replaces Delete Selected Record on the Table menu). When you select Table⇨Recall Selected Record, the mark in the Del column (at the left, next to the record number) is removed, indicating that the record is no longer marked for deletion.

More stuff

In order for this command to be available, you must be able to see those records that are marked for deletion — meaning that you have to have the Del column showing in your table. And *that* means that the easiest way to unmark a record is to just click the mark to remove it.

To recall a group of records, use Table⇨Table Utilities⇨Recall Records. To actually get rid of the records marked for deletion, use Table⇨Table Utilities⇨Pack Records. To find out about the Deleted setting, see Properties⇨Desktop.

Table⇨Replace Records

Lets you find text in your document and change it to something else. This command is most useful when you need to update the same value in several records.

For keyboard krazies

Just the facts

When you select Table⇨Replace Records, you get the Replace Records dialog box shown here. The whole point of this dialog box is to find matching text and replace it with something else. (I call this a search-and-replace mission.) The first part of the process — finding the records — is the same as that described for Table⇨Find Records, and I'm not going to repeat myself.

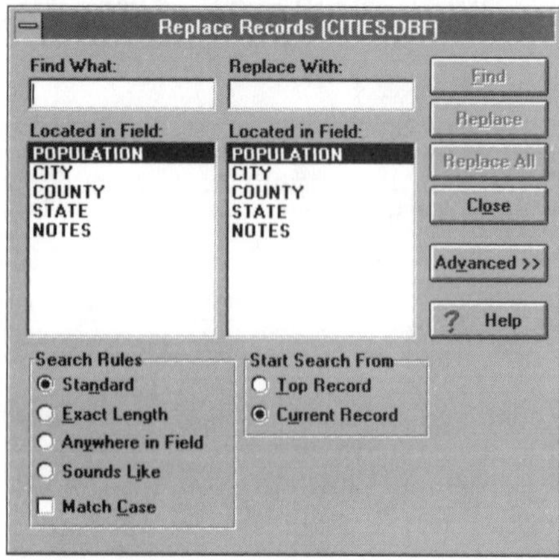

The most important change to the dialog box (from the one you get with Table⇨Find Records) is the Replace With box and its associated Located in Field list. This second list makes the Replace Records dialog box much more powerful. Now you can search for a match in one field and replace the contents of another field. For example, the area code for Vancouver, Washington, is changing later this year. If your database were set up to allow it, you could search for *Vancouver* in the CITY field and replace the contents of the AREA_CODE field with the new area code. The major weakness in the Replace Records feature is that you must replace *all* of the field's contents.

With the Replace Records dialog box, you have two choices in addition to the Find button: Replace and Replace All. Use the Find button to move to the first record that matches the text. When you are at a record with matching text, you can use the Replace button to make the change and then move to the next match.

The effect of the Replace All button depends on the settings controlled by the Advanced button. If you select Advanced, the dialog box expands to the one shown here.

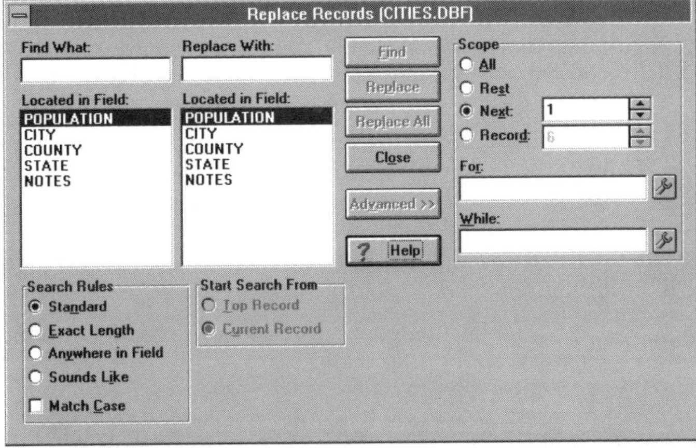

If the dialog box is not expanded, selecting Replace All causes the replacement specified to be made for every matching record. With the dialog box expanded, you can use the Scope section to control which records are changed. If All is selected, every matching record is changed. If Rest is selected, any matching records between the current record and the end of the table are changed. If Next is selected, you can enter the number of matching records following the current one that you want changed. With the Rest or Next options, the current record is always checked; if it matches, the replacement is made. You can use the Record option to check a single record (based on record number), although this is somewhat uncommon.

You can also use the For and While expressions to select which records are changed. If you enter an expression in the For box, only records that make the expression true are considered for replacement. This means that you can use a For expression to further restrict which records are changed. With a While expression, the search only continues until the expression is no longer true. You can combine either a For or a While expression with a Rest option or a Next value to restrict even further the number of records that are changed.

After dBASE has completed its changes, you see a dialog box listing how many changes were made and asking whether to commit the changes. If more changes are reported than you expected, you may want to select No and double-check the settings in the Replace Records dialog box. Once you select Yes, undoing the changes is very difficult.

More stuff

As with Table⇨Find Records, you can use expressions in both the Find What and Replace With boxes. By using an expression, you can replace the value of one field with that of another or with the results of a calculation involving the values of other fields.

If you are replacing numeric values and the new value does not fit in the field, you lose the old value anyway. If you have any doubts, check the width of the numeric field before trying to replace any of its values.

For a bit more on search-and-replace missions, see Chapter 11 in *dBASE For Windows For Dummies*.

The For and While scope expressions are further covered in the Glossary.

Table⇨Table Utilities⇨Append Records from File

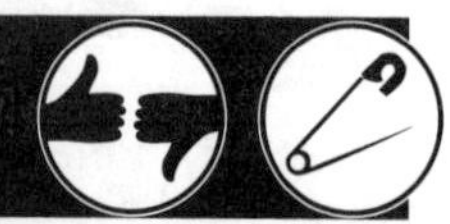

Imports records from another file into the current table. The other file can be a dBASE table, a Paradox file, a file with fixed-length fields, or a file where the fields are separated by a special character (called a delimiter). In order for this command to work, the names for the fields you want to import must match those in the current table.

Just the facts

The first thing you need to do is make sure that you know the location and format of the file containing the data you want to import. When you select Table⇨Table Utilities⇨Append Records from File, you get a dialog box asking for the format and the location — that's why I said you need to know that stuff. Put the location of the file into the File Name box (or use the button at the right end to open a dialog box where you can select the file) and then select the proper format for the file.

Your choices for file formats are a dBASE file, a Paradox file, SDF, or Delimited. The first two are pretty easy to understand; just find out which program created the file. With an SDF file, each field is of a fixed length (or, to put it another way, each field starts in the same column). With a Delimited file, each field is separated by the same symbol (often a comma). When you select a Delimited file format, you have to enter in the Delimiter box the symbol used to separate the fields.

Once you've entered the information describing the file, you may use the For box to enter an expression for selecting which records to import. Only those records that make the expression true will be added to the table. Leave the For box blank if you want to import all the records from the file.

When everything is set, select OK and sit back. The records that match the For expression are added to the end of the current table.

More stuff

Whether you import records marked for deletion is controlled by the Deleted setting in the Table category under Properties⇨Desktop. If the setting is cleared, records marked for deletion are imported and marked. Otherwise, they are not imported.

To import a field from a spreadsheet, use File⇨Import. The For scope expressions are further covered in the Glossary.

Table⇨Table Utilities⇨Calculate Records

Provides a quick way of calculating some basic statistics based upon values for some or all of the records in your table. You can do things such as find the total or average for a field without having to create a report to do it.

Just the facts

When you select Table⇨Table Utilities⇨Calculate Records, you get the dialog box shown here. The Fields list displays all the fields that can be used with the operation selected in the Calculation group. For example, if Average is selected, only fields with numeric values are listed. On the other hand, if Minimum is selected, all the fields with actual values are listed (OLE, binary, and memo fields are not included).

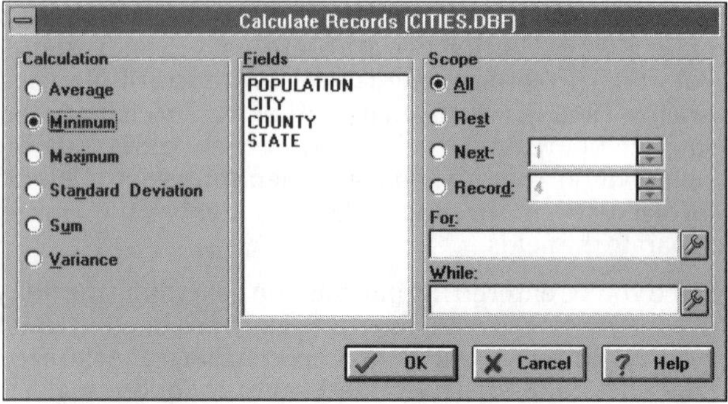

You can only perform one type of calculation at a time, but you can calculate for more than one field. First select the type of calculation and then select the fields. To select more than one field, hold down the Ctrl key while you click the additional fields. If you add a field you want to remove, hold down the Ctrl key and click it again to remove it from the group.

Once you've selected the type of calculation and the fields to be used, you can use the Scope area to select the records to be used in the calculation. If All is selected, then all the records in the table will be used. With Rest selected, only those records from the current record through the end of the table will be included. The Next option uses only the number of records you specify. The Record option is pretty useless because it uses only the record you specify. It's faster just to go to that record and look at the values (use Table⇨Go to Record Number). You can also use a For expression to create a rule for selecting records: only those records that make the expression true are included in the calculation. With a While expression, the calculation starts with the current record and continues until the While expression is no longer true. Often, you combine a For expression with either the Rest or the Next option.

After you select OK, dBASE does all the calculations and then displays a dialog box with the results.

More stuff

If you just want to know how many records you have, use Table⇨Table Utilities⇨Count. The For and While scope expressions are further covered in the Glossary.

Table⇨Table Utilities⇨ Close All Tables

Closes all the open tables without closing any of the other windows or exiting the program. This is a fast way of clearing out what you're working with.

Just the facts

If you're working with a bunch of tables, select Table⇨Table Utilities⇨Close All Tables and watch them all close up shop. Only those tables displayed in separate windows are closed. Any tables that are opened as part of a form or report are still available, but only within the form or report.

More stuff

If you're working with any forms, however, selecting Form⇨Table Utilities⇨Close All Tables causes the form you are working with to close the table it uses. This causes the fields to display the form object names (rather than the field contents), and the form is no longer usable. It's better to just use File⇨Close, which works with both forms and tables.

Table⇨Table Utilities⇨Close Table

Closes the current table.

Just the facts

If you're working with a table, all you do is select Table⇨Table Utilities⇨Close Table and watch the table close.

More stuff

This command is also available as Form⇨Table Utilities⇨Close Table, but that command is not as useful. When you select Form⇨Table Utilities⇨Close Table, the table containing the information is closed, but the form itself remains open. The fields simply display the form object names, and the form is no longer usable. It's better to just use File⇨Close, which works with both forms and tables.

Table⇨Table Utilities⇨Count Records

Counts the number of records in your table. This command is most useful when you include a scope expression, which counts only those records that make the scope expression true.

Just the facts

When you select Table⇨Table Utilities⇨Count Records, you get a dialog box where you can set a scope expression. The simplest choices are to count All the records or the Rest of the records (from the current record to the end of the table). You can combine any of the options with a For or While expression to select only those records that make the expression true. With a For expression, you generally use a Next value (which selects *that many* records, including the current one) or specify that the expression applies to All the records or only the Rest of the records. A While expression starts counting with the current record and keeps counting until the expression is no longer true.

Once you've created the expression to define the record count, select OK, and dBASE displays a dialog box showing the total number of records that were counted based on the rules in the scope expression.

More stuff

To perform quick calculations using the contents of fields, use Table⇨Table Utilities⇨Count Records.

Table⇨Table Utilities⇨ Delete Records

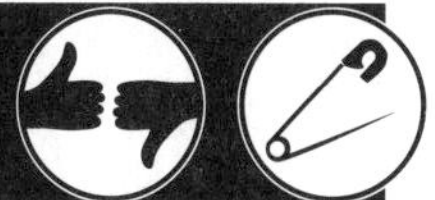

Lets you use a scope expression to delete a group of records. This command is great for cleaning up your database but can result in loss of data if you make a mistake.

Just the facts

When you select Table⇨Table Utilities⇨Delete Records, you get a dialog box where you can set a scope expression. The expression you enter is used to select which records to mark for deletion. Unless you want to clear out the entire database, you probably don't want to select All without completing the For or While portions of the expression. Without a limitation, All causes all the records in the table to be marked. It's almost as unlikely that you would use Rest by itself, which would remove the records from the current record to the end of the table. And there really isn't a good reason at all to use Record. If you want to delete a single record, just move to that record (with Table⇨Go to Record Number), check to make sure it's the right record, and then delete it with Table⇨Delete Selected Record.

You may in some cases want to use Next to delete a group of records starting with the current record, but most of the time you should create either a For or a While expression. With a For expression, you describe which record you want to get rid of and then specify that the expression applies to All the records or only the Rest of the records. A While expression starts deleting with the current record and keeps deleting records until the expression is no longer true. You can combine a While expression with a Next value to limit the number of records that are checked.

More stuff

When you use a Delete command, dBASE doesn't really delete the records immediately. Instead, the records are marked for deletion and are only removed when you use Table⇨Table Utilities⇨Pack Records.

You can use Table⇨Delete Selected Record to get rid of a single record and Table⇨TableUtilities⇨Recall Records to bring records back from the grave. (OK, it only unmarks them, but the effect is similar.)

Table⇨Table Utilities⇨ Export Records

Creates a separate file (in the format you request) and fills the file with values from the selected records. The point of this is to create a file you can use with another program.

Just the facts

When you select Table⇨Table Utilities⇨Export Records, you get what looks like a rather complex dialog box, but fortunately, it's quite easy to use. The dialog box has three portions: the Export File, the Scope Expression, and the field lists.

Probably the first things you should do are give the file a name and pick a file format. Type the name in the File Name box (or use the button at the right end of the field to open a Save As dialog box). Your choices for file formats are a dBASE file, a Paradox file, DBMEMO3, SDF, or Delimited. The first two are pretty easy to understand: just decide which program needs to be able to read the file. DBMEMO3 creates a file format compatible with dBASE III+. If you create an SDF file, each field is of a fixed length (or, to put it another way, each field starts in the same column). With a Delimited file, each field is separated by the same symbol (often a comma). When you select a Delimited file format, you have to enter in the Delimiter box the symbol used to separate the fields.

Next, it makes sense to select which fields are going to be included in the file. When you first open the dialog box, all the fields are listed under Selected Fields. If you want to remove a single field, highlight the field and click the button with the single arrowhead pointing to the left (<). To clear out all the fields and build the list yourself, just click the button with the double arrowhead pointing to the left (<<).The buttons that point to the right are used to add a field (>) or all the fields (>>) to the Selected Fields list. When you move a field, it is placed after the field currently selected in the list. The fields listed in the Selected Fields list (and only those fields) are put into the new file in the order listed.

Finally, you can create a scope expression to limit which records are put into the new file. You can select All the records or the Rest of the records (starting with the current record and moving to the end of the file), enter a number for the Next value (which causes *that many* records, starting with the current record, to be exported), or enter a record number for Record (though why you'd want to export a single record is a question I'd rather not think about). You can also create a For expression describing the records to export or a While expression, which means to export until the While expression is no longer true. You can combine For and While expressions with any of the other options to further control which records are put into the new file.

To create your new file, select OK and stand back. Faster than you can say *sdkslkjero*, the new file is created. (No, that's not a word, but exporting isn't all that fast, either.)

More stuff

If the Deleted option in the Tables category of Properties⇨Desktop is checked, records marked for deletion are not exported.

To bring files into dBASE, use Table⇨Append Records from File. The For and While scope expressions are further covered in the Glossary.

Table⇨Table Utilities⇨ Generate Records

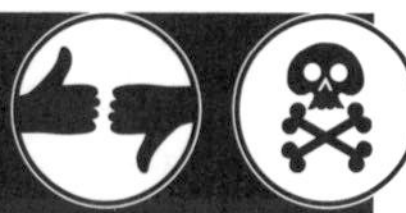

Creates a bunch of records at the end of your table filled with random values. Oddly enough, this isn't that useful a command, except to some nerdy types who use it to test forms and reports. You'll probably never need to use it.

Table⇨Table Utilities⇨ Manage Indexes

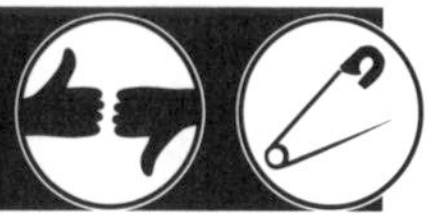

Creates, modifies, or deletes indexes for the current file. I've referred you here from several other places (such as Structure⇨Manage Indexes and Query⇨Manage Indexes), and it would be sorta fun to go ahead and send you somewhere else, but my editor won't let me. So, this is where I finally explain the mysteries of indexing.

Just the facts

An index is a special file that contains organized information about the contents of a field or combination of fields. You can think of the index file as containing a sorted list of all the values that appear in the field, with notes as to which records contain each value. Because the information in the index is organized, searching for a value in that field is faster. When you search for a value in a field that has an index, dBASE quickly locates the value in the sorted indexed file and then moves from the index back to the proper record in the table (because each value listed in the index also shows which record contains the value). In addition, one of your indexes is used to sort the table when the table is displayed.

Your first thought might be that if this process speeds up searches, why doesn't dBASE index all fields? The reason is that the index files take up additional space, and, in general, having more indexes causes dBASE to do more work managing them, which in turn slows down everything within dBASE (not just searches).

The standard rule is that you should index a field if it contains different values for most records and if it is a field you often use in searches. In some cases, you need to create a complex index that combines values from two or more fields. A complex index is particularly useful if you usually search those fields in combination (such as FIRST_NAME and LAST_NAME). Finally, if you search a certain subset of your records often, you can create an index for just those records.

When you select Table⇨Table Utilities⇨Manage Indexes, you get the Manage Indexes dialog box, which lists all current indexes. To create a new index, select Create. To change the characteristics of an index, select the index and then select Modify. With either option, you get the dialog box shown here, except that the title of one version is labeled Create Index and the other is Modify Index. (To get rid of an index, select it and then select Delete.)

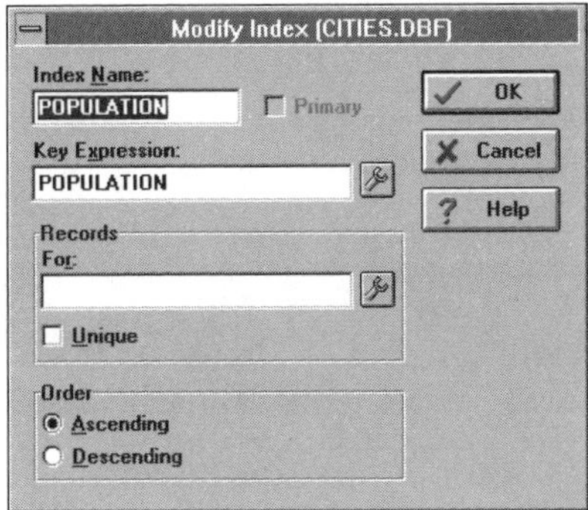

Use the Index Name box to give the index a name or to change the name of an existing index. Use the Key Expression box to indicate which field or fields should be used for an index. For a simple index, you can just enter the name of a field. For a complex index, you may use a formula to change the format of the values before indexing or create a formula combining the values of two or more fields. You should also select an order for the index — either Ascending (from smallest to largest) or Descending (from largest to smallest).

The Records section of the dialog box contains two very different options. The Unique option should be cleared if you want dBASE to index each record even if the current record contains the same value as the index field. Put a check next to Unique if you only want dBASE to index the record the first time it finds a particular value. The For box can be used to create a scope expression that selects the records to be indexed.

When you are done creating or modifying your index, select OK. This returns you to the Manage Indexes dialog box. Select the index you want to use to sort the table and then select OK. If you want the records to be listed by record number (rather than one of the indexed fields), select Natural Order. Your table returns to the screen. dBASE reindexes the tables and, if necessary, sorts the information using the new index.

More stuff

You can also create simple indexes while designing your table. At the end of the table structure grid is a column labeled Index. Originally, the value for the Index column is set to None, indicating that the field isn't indexed. To index a field, simply select either Ascend (for an ascending index) or Descend (for a descending index) from the list.

For another view on using indexes, see Chapter 15 in *dBASE For Windows For Dummies*.

You can also sort your table by using Table⇨Table Utilities⇨Sort Records. For more on For, see the Glossary.

Table⇨Table Utilities⇨ Pack Records

Actually gets rid of the records marked for deletion and updates the record numbers.

Just the facts

Even though this is one of the most dangerous commands in dBASE, there really isn't much to it. Select Table⇨Table Utilities⇨Pack Records, and dBASE removes any records that are marked for deletion. No warning. No dialog box.

More stuff

Unless you are very confident about what you're doing, you should always check the records that you intend to delete. To view those records that are marked for deletion, make sure that the Deleted option is cleared in the Table category of Properties⇨Desktop.

Use Table⇨Delete Selected Record and Table⇨Table Utilities⇨Delete Records to mark records for deletion. Use Table⇨Recall Selected Record or Table⇨Table Utilities⇨Recall Records to recover records deleted accidentally prior to packing the database.

Table⇨Table Utilities⇨ Recall Records

Recovers records that are marked for deletion. You can only use this command before packing the database (which actually removes the marked records).

Just the facts

When you delete a record in dBASE, you actually just mark it for deletion. You can recover it at any point until you pack the table. To start, you need to be able to see the deleted records. To do that, make sure that the Deleted option in the Table category of Properties⇨Desktop is cleared. In Browse view, you should see a column labeled Del right next to the record number (at the left of the record). A record with a red X in the Del column is marked for deletion. (You can clear the X — that is, recall the record — by clicking it.)

When you select Table⇨Table Utilities⇨Recall Records, you get a dialog box where you can create a scope expression for selecting which records to recall. Select All to have all the marked records recalled. Use Rest to recover all the marked records from the current record to the end of the file. To recall a certain number of records, starting with the current record, enter a number for the Next value. Alternatively, you can enter a record number for Record, although there are easier ways to recall a single record.

For greater control over which records are recalled, you can also create a For expression describing the records to recall or a While expression to keep recalling records until the While expression is no longer true. You can combine For and While expressions with any of the other options to further control which records are brought back from the brink of the grave.

More stuff

To really *remove* the marked records, use Table⇨Table Utilities⇨Pack Records. To recall a single record, move to the record and select Table⇨Recall Selected Record. To delete an individual record, use Table⇨Delete Selected Record. Table⇨Table Utilities⇨Delete Records deletes an entire group. For more on the Deleted option, see Properties⇨Desktop. The For and While scope expressions are further covered in the Glossary.

Table⇨Table Utilities⇨Reindex

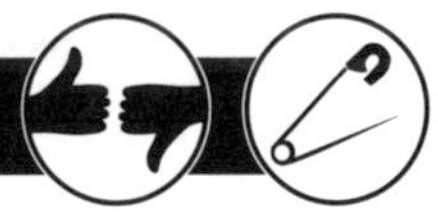

Updates the indexes for the current table. You may need to do this if you've changed the values in your indexed fields. If you are going to search your database or run a report based on a query, reindexing beforehand is always a good idea.

Just the facts

All there is to the Table⇨Table Utilities⇨Reindex command is selecting it.

More stuff

To find out about indexes, see Table⇨Table Utilities⇨Manage Indexes.

Table⇨Table Utilities⇨Sort Records

Creates a new table with the selected fields from the selected records in the order you requested. And you thought this was just about putting your table in order. No, that's Table⇨Table Utilities⇨Manage Indexes.

Just the facts

When you select Table⇨Table Utilities⇨Sort Records, you get a dialog box with several sections, the most important of which is Target Table. That's where you provide the Name for the new table. You can select between creating a dBASE table and a Paradox table.

You can use the Field Selection section to pick which fields are used to sort the new tables. Records are sorted on the first field in the Key Fields list, and then any records with identical entries for the first field are sorted on the second field. This process continues until all the records are sorted or until dBASE runs out of fields in the Key Fields list. To move a single record to the Key Fields list, select it and select the button with a single arrowhead pointing to the right (>). To remove a field from the Key Fields list, select it and select the button with the single arrowhead pointing to the left (<). The double arrowheads move all the fields from one list to the other.

The Scope section can be used to select a group of records to be put into the new table. The All option copies all the records from the current table. The Rest option copies the current record and all the records to the end of the table. A Next value starts copying with the current record and copies the number of records specified. If you want to, you can use the Record choice to copy a single record by record number. All of these options can be combined with a For expression (which copies only those records that make the expression true) or a While expression (which starts with the current record and continues copying until the expression is no longer true).

More stuff

If you copy only some of the records from the current table into the sorted table, you should probably keep both tables. If you copy all the records, however, you generally get rid of the original table. To do that, select it in the Navigator and use Edit⇨Delete.

To find out more about sorting, see Chapter 15 in *dBASE For Windows For Dummies*.

To just change the order of the records in the current table, use Table⇨Table Utilities⇨Manage Indexes.

Table⇨Table Utilities⇨ Zap Records

Evil, dangerous, bad command. Immediately, without regret, removes all the records in the current table. You do get a bit of warning, but if you answer Yes, all the records are gone.

Just the facts

Right after you select Table⇨Table Utilities⇨Zap Records, dBASE asks if you want to get rid of all the records in the table. Your choices are Yes and No. *Yes* means throw out all of that information you worked so hard to create. *No* means that it was all a mistake and you really don't mean to destroy everything. Don't ask me why this command exists — I haven't a clue.

More stuff

If you want to get rid of a group of records, use Table⇨Table Utilities⇨Delete Records instead. It marks the records for deletion, which gives you an opportunity to review what you're doing. You can then use Table⇨Table Utilities⇨Pack Records to actually remove the marked records from the file.

Table⇨Top Record

Jumps to the first record in the table. Once you're there, what you do is up to you.

For keyboard krazies

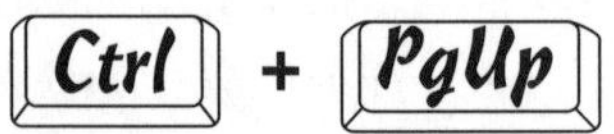

For mouse maniacs

Click this button to move to the first record in the table.

Just the facts

Select Table⇨Top Record to move to the start of the table.

More stuff

To jump to the beginning of the table, use Table⇨Bottom Record. Table⇨Next Record moves you down one record, and Table⇨Next Page moves you down one screen-full of records. Table⇨Previous Record moves you one record toward the start of the table, and Table⇨Previous Page moves you one screen-full of records in the same direction. If you know the record number, you can use Table⇨Go to Record Number to jump to a specific record.

Table⇨Unlock Selected Record

Releases your control over the selected record so that other people who are also using the file can make changes to it.

For keyboard krazies

Just the facts

You only see this command when two conditions are true: you are working in a network environment where other people can use the same database table at the same time, and you have locked a record with Table⇨Lock Selected Record so that only you can make changes to it. Use Table⇨Unlock Selected Record to let others have access to the record.

View⇨All

Displays all of the available dBASE items.

For mouse maniacs

This button is located on the left of the Navigator window and any catalog windows.

Just the facts

When you select View⇨All in the Navigator, dBASE lists any files with recognized extensions that are found in the current directory and, if active, along the search path. In a catalog, selecting View⇨All displays all items that have been added to the catalog. The easiest way to use the command is to click the All icon in the Navigator or catalog window.

More stuff

Two properties are very important in controlling what you see in the Navigator. The Search Path is only displayed when the Use Supplemental Search Path option under Properties⇨Navigator is checked. When Use Supplemental Search Path is cleared, only the current directory is searched for files to list. The Older File Types option in the Files category under Properties⇨Desktop controls whether dBASE lists older format files (from dBASE IV, for example) in both the Navigator and in catalogs. If Older File Types is checked, both older and newer files are displayed together in the window; otherwise, only files in a dBASE 5.0 format are displayed.

View⇨All, View⇨Forms, View⇨Labels, View⇨Programs, View⇨Queries, View⇨Reports, and View⇨Tables can all be used to control what is displayed within the Navigator or a catalog, but it's much easier to just click the button at the left edge of the window. View⇨Catalogs, View⇨Custom, View⇨Images, and View⇨Sounds only work in the Navigator window, but again it's easier to use the buttons at the left. To control the format of the items, use View⇨Details, View⇨Small Icons, or View⇨Large Icons. To change the order of the items displayed, use View⇨Sort.

View⇨Associations

Changes the view in a catalog window so that each item lists its closest association. For example, tables list the form that can be used to view the table's contents, while reports list the table or query that they are based upon.

Just the facts

View⇨Associations is a toggle, which means that selecting the command changes the setting from on to off and vice versa. When you look at the View menu, if a check is located to the left of the Associations command, then you are currently viewing the associations within the catalog. To stop viewing associations, simply select View⇨Associations. If there is not check mark, then you are not viewing the associations, but can turn them on by selecting View⇨Associations.

More stuff

View⇨All, View⇨Forms, View⇨Labels, View⇨Programs, View⇨Queries, View⇨Reports, and View⇨Tables can all be used to control what is displayed within the catalog. To control the format of the items, use View⇨Small Icons or View⇨Large Icons. To change the order of the items displayed, use View⇨Sort.

View⇨Browse Layout

Switches from the current view to Browse view, where each field is shown in its own column and each record in its own row. Browse view is the only standard view that can display more than one record.

For mouse maniacs

One click on this button and you are in Browse view, where you can see more than one record at a time.

Just the facts

All you have to do is select View⇨Browse Layout, and you are looking at your records neatly arranged in rows and columns. Kinda looks like a spreadsheet, doesn't it?

More stuff

A shortcut key (F2) exists to move you among the three layouts (Browse, Columnar, and Form), but it works a bit differently from most shortcuts. When you press F2, you switch from one view to another. You move from Browse Layout to Form Layout to Columnar Layout and then back to Browse Layout. So the shortcut doesn't take you to a particular view, it just changes to the next view in the list.

To find out about working in the Browse Layout, see Chapters 5 and 6 in *dBASE For Windows For Dummies*.

The other two commands for changing how you are viewing a record are View⇨Columnar Layout and View⇨Form Layout.

View⇨Catalogs

Displays all of the catalogs that are found by the Navigator.

For mouse maniacs

The Catalogs button is located on the left of the Navigator window; clicking it displays only the catalogs.

Just the facts

Select View⇨Catalogs, and all that appears in the Navigator window are those catalogs you've created. Of course, just clicking the Catalogs button at the left of the Navigator window is easier.

More stuff

You really should get into the habit of using catalogs to organize your databases. It's far too easy to create so many items that you can't find what you're looking for. Using catalogs cuts down on that problem significantly.

The Search Path is only displayed when the Use Supplemental Search Path option under Properties⇨Navigator is checked. When Use Supplemental Search Path is cleared, only the current directory is searched for files to list.

View⇨All, View⇨Forms, View⇨Labels, View⇨Programs, View⇨Queries, View⇨Reports, and View⇨Tables can all be used to control what is displayed within the Navigator or a catalog, but

it's much easier to just click the button at the left edge of the window. View⇨Catalogs, View⇨Custom, View⇨Images, and View⇨Sounds only work in the Navigator window, but again it's easier to use the buttons at the left. To control the format of the items, use View⇨Details, View⇨Small Icons, or View⇨Large Icons. To change the order of the items displayed, use View⇨Sort.

View⇨Columnar Layout

Changes from the current way of viewing records to displaying each record on its own screen with each field having its own row. The name comes from the fact that the field names are in one column and the entries for the field are in a second column.

For mouse maniacs

Switches you to viewing your records one at a time in the Columnar Layout.

Just the facts

Just select View⇨Columnar Layout and watch the display change to the Columnar Layout. Each record is displayed individually, and each field has its own row.

More stuff

The shortcut key for changing between the three layouts (Browse, Columnar, and Form) works a bit differently from most shortcuts. When you press F2 (the shortcut key), you switch from one view to another. You move from Browse Layout to Form Layout to Columnar Layout and then back to Browse Layout. So the shortcut doesn't take you to a particular view; it just changes to the next view in the list.

The other two commands for changing how you view a record are View⇨Browse Layout and View⇨Form Layout.

View⇨Controls

Displays the tools for drawing controls onto your form. You couldn't create a form without this command.

Just the facts

The View⇨Controls command is a toggle, which means its setting changes from on to off and then back to on. If you look at the View menu and find a check next to the Controls command, it means that the window is opened somewhere on your screen. To get rid of the window, select View⇨Controls. If there isn't a check mark next to Controls, you can select View⇨Controls to display the Controls window.

More stuff

To find out more about creating a form, see Catalog⇨New Form. To find the Controls window once it's opened, see Window⇨List of Open Windows.

View⇨Custom

Limits the Navigator to displaying only custom controls. The one oddity is that you need to tell the Navigator which extensions to display.

For mouse maniacs

The Custom button is located on the left of the Navigator window.

Just the facts

When you select View⇨Custom (or click the Custom button at the left of the Navigator), you see whichever files match the extensions shown in the Custom Files box at the top of the dialog box. To list different files, position your cursor in the Custom Files box and enter the new extension. If you want to list several extensions, separate them by commas. An extension, by the way, is the three-letter code at the end of a filename that identifies the type of file. When you enter an extension, always start with an asterisk and a period (*.). If the extension is VBX, then you enter ***.VBX**.

More stuff

The Search Path is only displayed when the Use Supplemental Search Path option under Properties⇨Navigator is checked. When Use Supplemental Search Path is cleared, only the current directory is searched for files to list.

View⇨All, View⇨Forms, View⇨Labels, View⇨Programs, View⇨Queries, View⇨Reports, and View⇨Tables can all be used to control what is displayed within the Navigator or a catalog, but it's much easier to just click the button at the left edge of the window. View⇨Catalogs, View⇨Custom, View⇨Images, and View⇨Sounds only work in the Navigator window, but again it's easier to use the buttons at the left. To control the format of the items, use View⇨Details, View⇨Small Icons, or View⇨Large Icons. To change the order of the items displayed, use View⇨Sort.

View⇨Details

Changes the display so that the detailed information is displayed for each item (rather than just the item's icon). The information includes the size of the file and the date and time when the item was last saved.

Just the facts

Select View⇨Details to see a list of the files in the Navigator or catalog window. For each file, dBASE lists its name, its size, and when it was last saved.

More stuff

The Details view is not available if you are using View⇨Associations.

To change the order of the items displayed, use View⇨Sort. To view items as icons, you can use View⇨Small Icons or View⇨Large Icons. View⇨All, View⇨Forms, View⇨Labels, View⇨Programs, View⇨Queries, View⇨Reports, and View⇨Tables can all be used to control what is displayed within the Navigator or a catalog, but it's much easier to just click the button at the left edge of the window. View⇨Catalogs, View⇨Custom, View⇨Images, and View⇨Sounds only work in the Navigator window, but again it's easier to use the buttons at the left.

View⇨Enlarged

Gives you a magnified view of the report or labels that you are working with. This lets you see the detail on your reports or actually read what's on the labels.

Just the facts

Select View⇨Enlarged and watch the text get much bigger.

More stuff

The other commands for controlling the size of the display are View⇨Normal and View⇨Reduced.

View⇨Field Contents

Opens a binary, OLE, or memo field so that you can view the contents. Each of the field types displays an icon indicating what type of item is stored in the field. You can also view the results by double-clicking the field.

For keyboard krazies

Just the facts

OLE, binary, and memo fields do not display their contents when you are viewing the table. Instead, they display the icons shown here.

Empty OLE field

OLE field with something in it

Empty memo field

Memo field with text

Empty binary field

Binary field with Image

Binary field with sound

To see the contents of these types of fields, you must use a special viewer (such as the OLE Viewer, Image Viewer, Sound Player, or Text Editor). To open the viewer, you can select the icon that is shown in the field and select View⇨Field Contents (or just double-click the icon).

View⇨Form

Switches from designing the form to actually using it.

For keyboard krazies

For mouse maniacs

When a form is in the current window, this button moves you from the Form Designer to working with the form.

Just the facts

Simply select View⇨Form to change from designing the form to using it. You have to save any changes to the design before you can use the form.

More stuff

To move from using a form to making changes to the design, select View⇨Form Design.

View⇨Form Design

Displays the form in the Form Designer so that you can make changes to it.

For keyboard krazies

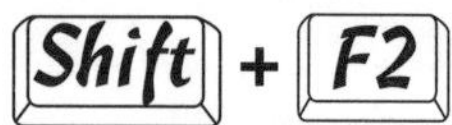

For mouse maniacs

When a form is opened in the window, this button moves you to the Form Designer.

Just the facts

All you need to do to switch from working with a form to working with its design is select View⇨Form Design.

More stuff

For more information about creating a form, use Catalog⇨New Form. To change back to working with the form, use View⇨Form.

View⇨Form Layout

Changes to viewing the records in the current table in the Form Layout view. Each record is displayed individually, with the fields arranged in groups across the screen.

For mouse maniacs

Clicking this button displays records one at a time in the Form Layout view.

Just the facts

To see the record as a form, select View⇨Form Layout.

More stuff

The shortcut key for changing between the three layouts (Browse, Columnar, and Form) works a bit differently from most shortcuts. When you press F2 (the shortcut key), you switch from one view to another. You move from Browse Layout to Form Layout to Columnar Layout and then back to Browse Layout. So the shortcut doesn't take you to a particular view; it just changes to the next view in the list.

The other two commands for changing how you are viewing a record are View⇨Browse Layout and View⇨Columnar Layout.

View⇨Forms

Changes the catalog or Navigator window so that it only displays forms.

For mouse maniacs

This button is located on the left of the Navigator window and any catalog windows.

Just the facts

Just select View⇨Forms, and all you see in the current window is a bunch of forms.

More stuff

When you are working with a catalog, you can select View⇨Associations so that each form is listed with its associated table or query. Unlike other association views, an associated form appears indented on the second line, and the associated table or query appears at the left margin on the line above. A line connects the two items to make the association even clearer.

Two properties are very important in controlling what you see in the Navigator. The Search Path is only displayed when the Use Supplemental Search Path option under Properties⇨Navigator is checked. When Use Supplemental Search Path is cleared, only the current directory is searched for files to list. The Older File Types option in the Files category under Properties⇨Desktop controls whether dBASE lists older format files (from dBASE IV, for example) in both the Navigator and in catalogs. If Older File Types is checked, both older and newer files are displayed together in the window; otherwise, only files in a dBASE 5.0 format are displayed.

View⇨All, View⇨Forms, View⇨Labels, View⇨Programs, View⇨Queries, View⇨Reports, and View⇨Tables can all be used to control what is displayed within the Navigator or a catalog, but it's much easier to just click the button at the left edge of the window. View⇨Catalogs, View⇨Custom, View⇨Images, and

View⇨Sounds only work in the Navigator window, but again it's easier to use the buttons at the left. To control the format of the items, use View⇨Details, View⇨Small Icons, or View⇨Large Icons. To change the order of the items displayed, use View⇨Sort.

View⇨Images

Restricts the Navigator window to displaying only files that contain images stored in a PCX or BMP format.

For mouse maniacs

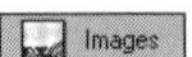

This button is located on the left of the Navigator window.

Just the facts

Select View⇨Images or click the Images button at the left of the window; the Navigator then displays only those items that contain figures stored in a PCX or BMP format.

More stuff

Within a table, to view the contents of a binary file that contains an image, use View⇨Field Contents or double-click the field.

The Search Path is only displayed when the Use Supplemental Search Path option under Properties⇨Navigator is checked. When Use Supplemental Search Path is cleared, only the current directory is searched for files to list.

View⇨All, View⇨Forms, View⇨Labels, View⇨Programs, View⇨Queries, View⇨Reports, and View⇨Tables can all be used to control what is displayed within the Navigator or a catalog, but it's much easier to just click the button at the left edge of the window. View⇨Catalogs, View⇨Custom, View⇨Images, and View⇨Sounds only work in the Navigator window, but again it's easier to use the buttons at the left. To control the format of the items, use View⇨Details, View⇨Small Icons, or View⇨Large Icons. To change the order of the items displayed, use View⇨Sort.

View⇨Labels

Changes the list to show only files of labels.

For mouse maniacs

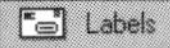

The Labels button is located on the left of the Navigator window and any catalog windows.

Just the facts

You can either select View⇨Labels or click the Labels button to restrict the display to files that contain Crystal Reports labels.

More stuff

When you are working with a catalog, you can select View⇨Associations so that each label file lists its associated table or query. The label item appears in the left column, and the report or query is indented on the line below. A line connects the two items to make the association even clearer.

Two properties are very important in controlling what you see in the Navigator. The Search Path is only displayed when the Use Supplemental Search Path option under Properties⇨Navigator is checked. When Use Supplemental Search Path is cleared, only the current directory is searched for files to list. The Older File Types option in the Files category under Properties⇨Desktop controls whether dBASE lists older format files (from dBASE IV, for example) in both the Navigator and in catalogs. If Older File Types is checked, both older and newer files are displayed together in the window; otherwise, only files in a dBASE 5.0 format are displayed.

View⇨All, View⇨Forms, View⇨Labels, View⇨Programs, View⇨Queries, View⇨Reports, and View⇨Tables can all be used to control what is displayed within the Navigator or a catalog, but it's much easier to just click the button at the left edge of the window. View⇨Catalogs, View⇨Custom, View⇨Images, and View⇨Sounds only work in the Navigator window, but again it's easier to use the buttons at the left. To control the format of the items, use View⇨Details, View⇨Small Icons, or View⇨Large Icons. To change the order of the items displayed, use View⇨Sort.

View⇨Large Icons

Changes the display so that the icons are a bit larger. This is great for those of us who have trouble seeing the normal icons. Unfortunately, the text size stays the same.

Just the facts

Select View⇨Large Icons to have slightly bigger icons.

More stuff

You can change the spacing between icons by using Properties⇨Catalog Window or Properties⇨Navigator (depending on whether you're in a catalog window or working with the Navigator).

The other commands to control the format of what you see are View⇨Details and View⇨Small Icons. To change the order of the items displayed, use View⇨Sort. View⇨All, View⇨Forms, View⇨Labels, View⇨Programs, View⇨Queries, View⇨Reports, and View⇨Tables can all be used to control what is displayed within the Navigator or a catalog, but it's much easier to just click the button at the left edge of the window. View⇨Catalogs, View⇨Custom, View⇨Images, and View⇨Sounds only work in the Navigator window, but again it's easier to use the buttons at the left.

View⇨Layout View

Changes to the standard Design view for creating, modifying, and deleting controls on a form. You only need to use this command when you have used View⇨Order View to change to the special Form Designer view that is used for controlling how you move between items on the form.

For mouse maniacs

Click this button to change the Form Designer to Layout View.

Just the facts

The Form Designer actually has design views: Order and Layout.

Layout view is used for working with the controls that appear on the form in terms of their look and function. Order view is used to determine how the user of the form moves between the items. To move from Order view to Layout view, select View⇨Layout View.

More stuff

To find out what you can do in Layout view, see Catalog⇨New Form. For more on working in the Order view, see View⇨Order View.

View⇨Normal

Displays the report or set of labels in a life-size format.

Just the facts

Select View⇨Normal to see your report or label file displayed in a size that closely matches what you'll get from your printer.

More stuff

Your other two choices are View⇨Enlarged and View⇨Reduced.

View⇨Object Properties

Displays the Properties window for the controls on a form. You need to have this window available to control how the controls look and function.

Just the facts

Simply select View⇨Object Properties to open the Properties window. You only need to do this once for each design session. After that — unless you close it for some reason — the Properties window is listed on the Windows menu.

More stuff

To find out a bit about how you use the Properties window, see Catalog⇨New Form.

View⇨Order View

Changes the Form Designer into Order view, where you can set the order in which the user of the form will move between items. When you move into Order view, the buttons on the SpeedBar change. The other Form Designer view is Layout view, which you get by selecting View⇨Layout View.

For mouse maniacs

Click this button to change to the Order view within the Form Designer.

When you move into Order view, the controls for controlling the layers of the form disappear and you get this Order control instead.

Just the facts

You select View⇨Order View when you have almost completed your form and are ready to refine how the form's users will move between the controls on the form. There are two ways to use the Order control. The easier method is to click the reset button (the portion of the control with the arrow pointing to the number 1) and then click the controls in the same order that you want the user to move between them. The first control you select is the one where the user will start when using the form.

The other method for using the Order control is to set a value (using the right-hand portion of the control) and click a control, which changes that control to the position equal to that value in the sequence. All of the other controls are renumbered to adjust for the changed number.

After changing the tab order, you may need to return to the Layout view to adjust which fields are hidden by other fields.

More stuff

For more on creating a new form, see Catalog⇨New Form.

View⇨Procedures

Displays the Procedure Editor when you're working with the Form Designer or designing menus. (Unless you change it, the Procedure Editor is just the plain dBASE Text Editor.) You only need to use this command if you're writing your own programs and procedures, so I'm not going to discuss it. OK, I will mention that you can get rid of the Procedure Editor by selecting View⇨Procedures.

View⇨Programs

Limits the Navigator (or the current catalog) to displaying only programs.

For mouse maniacs

This button is located on the left of the Navigator window and any catalog windows.

Just the facts

You can either select View⇨Programs or click the Programs button at the left of the window. They both restrict the list to showing only programs.

More stuff

The Search Path is only displayed when the Use Supplemental Search Path option under Properties⇨Navigator is checked. When Use Supplemental Search Path is cleared, only the current directory is searched for files to list.

View⇨All, View⇨Forms, View⇨Labels, View⇨Programs, View⇨Queries, View⇨Reports, and View⇨Tables can all be used to control what is displayed within the Navigator or a catalog, but it's much easier to just click the button at the left edge of the window. View⇨Catalogs, View⇨Custom, View⇨Images, and View⇨Sounds only work in the Navigator window, but again it's easier to use the buttons at the left. To control the format of the items, use View⇨Details, View⇨Small Icons, or View⇨Large Icons. To change the order of the items displayed, use View⇨Sort.

View⇨Queries

Displays only queries within the current window.

For mouse maniacs

This button is located on the left of the Navigator window and any catalog windows.

Just the facts

Just select View⇨Queries (or click the Queries button at the left of the window), and all you see is a list of the queries.

More stuff

When you're working with a catalog, you can select View⇨Associations so that each query lists any associated report or label file. The query appears in the left column, and the report or label file is indented on the line below. A line connects the two items to make the association even clearer.

Two properties are very important in controlling what you see in the Navigator. The Search Path is only displayed when the Use Supplemental Search Path option under Properties⇨Navigator is checked. When Use Supplemental Search Path is cleared, only the current directory is searched for files to list. The Older File Types option in the Files category under Properties⇨Desktop controls whether dBASE lists older format files (from dBASE IV, for example) in both the Navigator and in catalogs. If Older File Types is checked, both older and newer files are displayed together in the window; otherwise, only files in a dBASE 5.0 format are displayed.

View⇨All, View⇨Forms, View⇨Labels, View⇨Programs, View⇨Queries, View⇨Reports, and View⇨Tables can all be used to control what is displayed within the Navigator or a catalog, but it's much easier to just click the button at the left edge of the window. View⇨Catalogs, View⇨Custom, View⇨Images, and View⇨Sounds only work in the Navigator window, but again it's easier to use the buttons at the left. To control the format of the items, use View⇨Details, View⇨Small Icons, or View⇨Large Icons. To change the order of the items displayed, use View⇨Sort.

View⇨Query Design

Changes viewing the results of a query to viewing the Query Designer. You use the Query Designer to make changes to your query.

For keyboard krazies

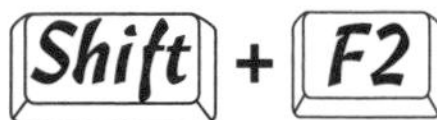

For mouse maniacs

When you are working with a query, clicking this button moves you to the Query Designer.

Just the facts

Select View⇨Query Design and you are suddenly (or maybe not so suddenly) in the Query Designer, where you can make changes to your query.

More stuff

To move back to using your query, use View⇨Query Results. For a description of creating a query, see Catalog⇨New Query.

View⇨Query Results

Displays a table containing the results of the current query.

For keyboard krazies

For mouse maniacs

When you are working with a query, clicking this button displays the results of the query.

Just the facts

This command actually displays the results of your query. Without it, you could never see the answer to your question. To move from the question in the Query Designer to the answer, just select View⇨Query Results.

More stuff

To move back to designing your query, use View⇨Query Design. For a description of creating a query, see Catalog⇨New Query.

View⇨Reduced

Shrinks the current report or page of labels so that you can see the entire page on-screen. This command is much more useful for reports, where you can get an idea of what the entire page looks like.

Just the facts

Just select View⇨Reduced and you get an *Alice in Wonderland* effect as the report just gets smaller.

More stuff

The other two commands for controlling the size of the display are View⇨Normal and View⇨Enlarged.

View⇨Reports

Causes the current window to display reports and only reports.

For mouse maniacs

This button is located on the left of the Navigator window and any catalog windows.

Just the facts

Just select View⇨Reports (or click the Reports button at the left of the window), and the list contains only reports. Of course, there are several types of reports, including a standard Crystal Reports report and Crystal Reports cross-tabs.

More stuff

Two properties are very important in controlling what you see in the Navigator. The Search Path is only displayed when the Use Supplemental Search Path option under Properties⇨Navigator is checked. When Use Supplemental Search Path is cleared, only the current directory is searched for files to list. The Older File Types option in the Files category under Properties⇨Desktop controls whether dBASE lists older format files (from dBASE IV, for example) in both the Navigator and in catalogs. If Older File Types is checked, both older and newer files are displayed together in the window; otherwise, only files in a dBASE 5.0 format are displayed.

View⇨All, View⇨Forms, View⇨Labels, View⇨Programs, View⇨Queries, View⇨Reports, and View⇨Tables can all be used to control what is displayed within the Navigator or a catalog, but it's much easier to just click the button at the left edge of the window. View⇨Catalogs, View⇨Custom, View⇨Images, and View⇨Sounds only work in the Navigator window, but again it's easier to use the buttons at the left. To control the format of the items, use View⇨Details, View⇨Small Icons, or View⇨Large Icons. To change the order of the items displayed, use View⇨Sort.

View⇨Small Icons

Changes the icons in the window to the smaller size. This is the view most commonly used in Windows programs.

Just the facts

Select View⇨Small Icons. It's one of those commands without a lot of options.

More stuff

You can change the spacing between icons by using Properties⇨Catalog Window or Properties⇨Navigator (depending on whether you're in a catalog window or working with the Navigator).

Other choices for controlling the format of the items are View⇨Details and View⇨Large Icons. To change the order of the items displayed, use View⇨Sort. View⇨All, View⇨Forms, View⇨Labels, View⇨Programs, View⇨Queries, View⇨Reports, and View⇨Tables can all be used to control what is displayed within the Navigator or a catalog, but it's much easier to just click the button at the left edge of the window. View⇨Catalogs, View⇨Custom, View⇨Images, and View⇨Sounds only work in the Navigator window, but again it's easier to use the buttons at the left.

View⇨Sort

Changes the order of the items displayed in a catalog window or in the Navigator. Whether you're looking at icons or details, the View⇨Sort command determines the order of the items. This command is a bit strange because in the Navigator, it's View⇨Sort (Alt, V, O); but when working with a catalog window, it's View⇨Sort (Alt, V, S).

Just the facts

To use the View⇨Sort command, you just need to select one of the four choices from the submenu that appears. Each of these choices organizes the window based on one of the file's characteristics.

The first, by Name, displays the items in alphabetical order. This is probably the order you will want to use most often.

The second choice, by Type and Extension, groups the items by their file extensions (the letters after the period in the filename) and therefore groups files of the same type. This option is most useful when you're viewing all item types together (with View⇨All) or when you have a mixture of old and new formats for your files.

The third option, by Size, lists the files from smallest to largest, which is useful when you are trying to free up space and need to find a large file to throw out.

The fourth option, by Date and Time, lists the files so that the one you worked with most recently is at the bottom of the list. This option can be very useful if you need to find the file you were working with yesterday but can't remember the name.

More stuff

To control the format of the items, use View⇨Details, View⇨Small Icons, or View⇨Large Icons. View⇨All, View⇨Forms, View⇨Labels, View⇨Programs, View⇨Queries, View⇨Reports, and View⇨Tables can all be used to control what is displayed within the Navigator or a catalog, but it's much easier to just click the button at the left edge of the window. View⇨Catalogs, View⇨Custom, View⇨Images, and View⇨Sounds only work in the Navigator window, but again it's easier to use the buttons at the left.

View⇨Sounds

Makes the Navigator show only sound files. You can only use these files if your computer has some way of playing sounds.

For mouse maniacs

This button is located on the left of the Navigator window.

Just the facts

Select View⇨Sounds (or click the Sounds button at the left of the Navigator) to limit the items in the Navigator window to sound files.

More stuff

Within a table, use View⇨Field Contents or double-click the field to hear the contents of a binary file that contains a sound.

The Search Path is only displayed when the Use Supplemental Search Path option under Properties⇨Navigator is checked. When Use Supplemental Search Path is cleared, only the current directory is searched for files to list.

View⇨All, View⇨Forms, View⇨Labels, View⇨Programs, View⇨Queries, View⇨Reports, and View⇨Tables can all be used to control what is displayed within the Navigator or a catalog, but it's much easier to just click the button at the left edge of the window. View⇨Catalogs, View⇨Custom, View⇨Images, and View⇨Sounds only work in the Navigator window, but again it's easier to use the buttons at the left. To control the format of the items, use View⇨Details, View⇨Small Icons, or View⇨Large Icons. To change the order of the items displayed, use View⇨Sort.

View⇨Table Records

Changes from looking at the table structure to viewing the actual contents of the table. You must save any changes to the structure before you can look at the table's contents.

For keyboard krazies

For mouse maniacs

If you are working with a table's structure, you can click this button to move to working with the contents of the table.

Just the facts

When you select View⇨Table Records, you are asked to save any changes to the structure. Once you've saved the changes (or thrown them out), you can look at the records in your table and make any changes you want.

More stuff

To add records to your table, use Table⇨Add Records.

View⇨Table Structure

Displays the structure of the table so that you can make changes to the field definitions. Perform this command only if you know how to design a database table.

For keyboard krazies

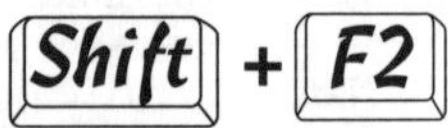

For mouse maniacs

If you are working with a table, click this button to view the table's structure.

Just the facts

Select View⇨Table Structure and you're no longer working with the contents of the table but with its structure. Be very careful, because changing the structure of an existing table can cause you to lose some of the information you worked so hard to put into the database. On the other hand, adding new fields is usually safe.

More stuff

For more on designing a table, see Catalog⇨New Table.

View⇨Tables

Displays only database tables in the current window.

For mouse maniacs

This button is located on the left of the Navigator window and any catalog windows.

Just the facts

Changing the contents of either a catalog window or the Navigator so that the only things on-screen are database tables is really quite easy. Just select View⇨Tables or click the Tables button at the left of the window.

More stuff

When you're working with a catalog, you can select View⇨Associations so that each table lists any forms based on that table. The table appears in the left column, and the form is indented on the line below. A line connects the two items to make the association even clearer.

Two properties are very important in controlling what you see in the Navigator. The Search Path is only displayed when the Use Supplemental Search Path option under Properties⇨Navigator is checked. When Use Supplemental Search Path is cleared, only the current directory is searched for files to list. The Older File Types option in the Files category under Properties⇨Desktop controls whether dBASE lists older format files (from dBASE IV, for example) in both the Navigator and in catalogs. If Older File Types is checked, both older and newer files are displayed together in the window; otherwise, only files in a dBASE 5.0 format are displayed.

View⇨All, View⇨Forms, View⇨Labels, View⇨Programs, View⇨Queries, View⇨Reports, and View⇨Tables can all be used to control what is displayed within the Navigator or a catalog, but it's much easier to just click the button at the left edge of the window. View⇨Catalogs, View⇨Custom, View⇨Images, and View⇨Sounds only work in the Navigator window, but again it's easier to use the buttons at the left. To control the format of the items, use View⇨Details, View⇨Small Icons, or View⇨Large Icons. To change the order of the items displayed, use View⇨Sort.

Window⇨1 Navigator

Moves you to the Navigator window.

For mouse maniacs

Clicking this button takes you immediately to the Navigator window.

Just the facts

No matter how many windows you have open or which one you are working with, the Navigator is always the first choice on the Windows menu. Just select Window⇨1 Navigator and you can open or delete items or use any of the commands on the Navigator.

More stuff

The Navigator lists all the items that it can find. Although this is convenient when you only have a few files, it can get overwhelming. That's why you should use catalogs to organize your material. Creating a new catalog is discussed under Navigator⇨New Catalog.

Window⇨2 Command

Moves you to the Command window, where you can work with dBASE as though it were a text-based program we know and love from the 1980s.

For mouse maniacs

Clicking this button moves you to the Command window, where you probably don't want to be.

Just the facts

Only the creators of dBASE could get away with calling this a feature. The Command window enables you to enter dBASE commands as text rather than selecting from a menu or using shortcuts. They did this because many dBASE programmers (read *nerds*) are used to typing their commands and aren't willing to learn a new way of doing things. Basically, the advertising ploy is something like "We invented a brand-new interface for using dBASE in Windows that you don't have to use." Go figure. Anyway, it's something a nice person like yourself can ignore.

Window⇨Arrange Icons

Organizes the icons for any minimized windows at the bottom of the dBASE window.

Just the facts

As soon as you select the command, any windows that have been reduced to icon will line up neatly in a row at the bottom. To see what I mean, take a look at the figure for Window⇨Tile Horizontally.

More stuff

To minimize a window to an icon, click the down-arrow in the upper-left corner of the window you want to minimize. To restore a window to normal size from an icon, double-click the icon.

Window⇨Cascade

Arranges all of the opened windows so that the edge of each is visible behind the next window.

For keyboard krazies

Just the facts

As soon as you select Window⇨Cascade, your windows are rearranged (as shown in the following figure).

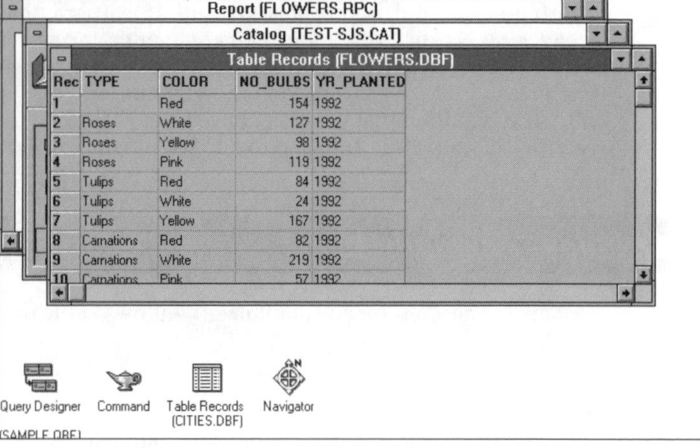

These windows are organized in a cascading fashion. No matter which one I pick, a little bit of each window will still be showing. Just click the visible part of the window to make it active and move it to the top of the pile.

More stuff

For other ways of arranging your windows, see Window⇨Tile Horizontally and Window⇨Tile Vertically.

Window⇨Close All Windows

Closes everything that you are working with except for the Navigator and the Command window. Everything is closed, whether it was an opened window or had been minimized as an icon. For a less drastic technique, use File⇨Close.

Window⇨List of Open Windows

Lets you choose which of the open windows you want to work with. In dBASE, the first item is always the Navigator and the second is always the Command window, but the other entries on the list represent windows that you have been working with.

Just the facts

To move to one of the windows on the list, simply select the name from the menu. (If you're using the keyboard, type the number in front of the name to select an item.) This feature is most useful when you have maximized your windows and can therefore only see one at a time. Otherwise, if part of the window that you want to work with is showing, you can just click that part of the window to make it active and move it to the front.

Window⇨Tile Horizontally

Arranges your windows so that they appear stacked.

Just the facts

Just select Window⇨Tile Horizontally to arrange the windows into separate tiles on the screen. Each window extends the full length of the screen, but the height depends on the number of windows that are open. The following example shows three windows:

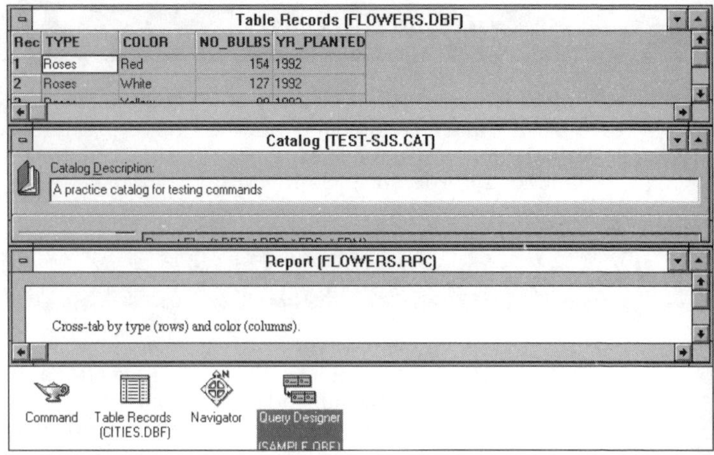

If you reduced any windows to icons, the tiling allows room to view the icons (as in the example). Unless both the Navigator and the Command window are opened, you'll always have this area for icons.

More stuff

To arrange your windows tiled in the other direction, use Window⇨Tile Vertically. For another approach entirely, see Window⇨Cascade.

Window⇨Tile Vertically

Arranges the open windows so that they appear side-by-side.

For keyboard krazies

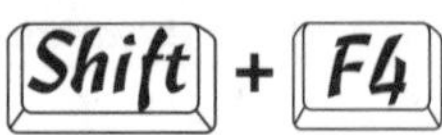

Just the facts

Just select Window⇨Tile Vertically to arrange the windows into separate, side-by-side tiles. Each window extends from the top of the dBASE window to just above the icons at the bottom. The width depends on the number of windows that are open. The following example shows three windows:

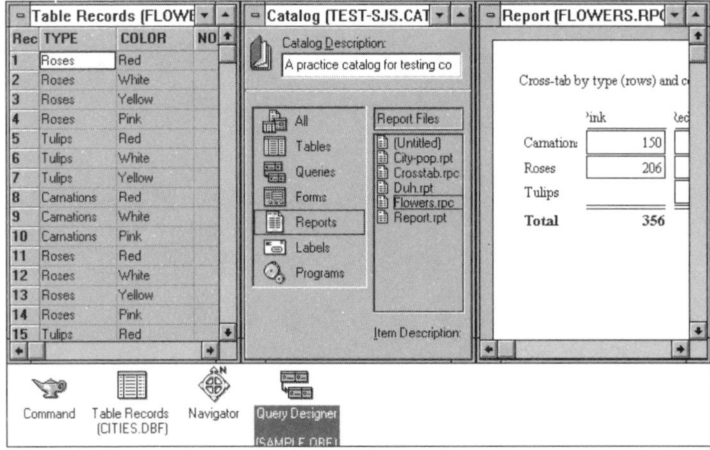

If you reduced any windows to icons, the tiling allows room to view the icons (as in the example). Unless both the Navigator and the Command window are opened, you'll always have this area for icons.

More stuff

To arrange your windows tiled in the other direction, use Window⇨Tile Horizontally. For another approach entirely, see Window⇨Cascade.

Stuart's Superior SpeedBar Survey

Stuart's Superior SpeedBar Survey

OK, in some of the other books, this is called *The Toolbar Tour*, but that's because most other programs call these things toolbars. Borland calls them SpeedBars, so you end up with a SpeedBar survey. It's superior because so far it's the only one, which means it's the best. For each toolbar — whoops, I mean SpeedBar — there's a brief description of when the SpeedBar is available, what it's used for, and a listing of all of the buttons on the SpeedBar. For each button, I've given the button a name, provided a brief description of its use, and the name of the command it is associated with.

The buttons on the various SpeedBars are one of the two most useful shortcuts in dBASE. The other shortcuts are the various SpeedMenus that appear when you click the right mouse button. If you find yourself doing the same task over and over, it's worth checking whether there is a SpeedBar button or a keyboard shortcut to activate the command. To find out, just look up the command in the Command Reference. If no button or keyboard shortcut exists, check whether the command appears on a SpeedMenu. As you go about doing the task, click the right mouse button and see what commands are available.

Catalog Window SpeedBar

You only see the Catalog Window SpeedBar when you are working with a catalog window. The most important thing to know about this SpeedBar is that the Use Item and Design Item buttons activate different commands depending upon what is selected. For example, if you have an existing form selected, the buttons are the same as Catalog⇨Run Form (for Use Item) and Catalog⇨Design Form (for Design Item). On the other hand, if you have the untitled form selected, the Design Item command is the same as Catalog⇨New Form (and the Use Item button isn't available).

New Item: Displays a menu where you can select what type of item to create (File⇨New).

Open: Opens the dialog box you use to select which file to open (File⇨Open).

Cut: Removes the selected text and puts it on the Clipboard (Edit⇨Cut).

Copy: Puts a copy of the selected text onto the Clipboard (Edit⇨Copy).

Paste: Inserts the contents of the Clipboard (Edit⇨Paste).

Use Item: Opens the selected item for use (one of the Catalog⇨Run items such as Catalog⇨Run Form).

Design Item: Opens the selected item in its designer. For example, a report is opened in Crystal Reports, and a form is opened in the Form Designer. (One of the Catalog⇨Design *item* commands such as Catalog⇨Design Form or, if you've selected an untitled item, one of the Catalog⇨New *item* commands such as Catalog⇨New Form.)

Add Item: Opens a dialog box that you can use to add an item to the current catalog (Catalog⇨Add Item).

Delete: Removes the selected item. When in a catalog window, the item is only removed from the catalog but remains on disk (Edit⇨Delete).

Navigator: Opens the Navigator so that you can work with your items (Window⇨1 Navigator).

Command window: Opens the Command window. You probably won't ever need to do this (Window⇨2 Command).

Form Expert: Opens the Form Expert for creating a new form. The process of creating a new form is described in Catalog⇨New Form (Help⇨Experts).

Interactive Tutor: Displays the first screen of the Interactive Tutors, where you can select a topic for dBASE to help you with (Help⇨Interactive Tutors).

Command Window SpeedBar

You only see this SpeedBar if you are working in the Command window, which isn't where you can type text commands for dBASE rather than use the menus and buttons. The only real use for this SpeedBar is to check sections of programming code, which is something I refuse to discuss.

New Item: Displays a menu where you can select what type of item to create (File⇨New).

Open: Opens the dialog box you use to select which file to open (File⇨Open).

Cut: Removes the selected text and puts it on the Clipboard (Edit⇨Cut).

Copy: Copies the selected text onto the Clipboard (Edit⇨Copy).

Paste: Inserts the contents of the Clipboard (Edit⇨Paste).

Do Selection: Tries to run the selected commands. This is beyond what is covered in this Quick Reference.

Do Program: Tries to run all of the commands within the program. This is beyond the scope of this book.

Debugger: Opens the dBASE debugger program where you can try to track down any errors in your program. This is an entirely separate program and isn't covered here.

Navigator: Opens the Navigator so that you can work with your items (Window⇨1 Navigator).

Command window: Opens the Command window. You probably won't ever need to do this (Window⇨2 Command).

Form Expert: Opens the Form Expert for creating a new form. The process of creating a new form is described in Catalog⇨New Form (Help⇨Experts).

Interactive Tutor: Displays the first screen of the Interactive Tutors where you can select a topic for dBASE to help you with (Help⇨Interactive Tutors).

Form Designer SpeedBar

You get this SpeedBar when you are designing a form. It's a bit unusual because it changes slightly depending upon what you are doing with the form design. The SpeedBar shown is what you see while you are creating or modifying controls in the Layout view. If you move to the Order view, then the Order control appears and replaces all of the buttons associated with the Layout menu. The Order control is listed here with notes about which commands appear or disappear as you switch views.

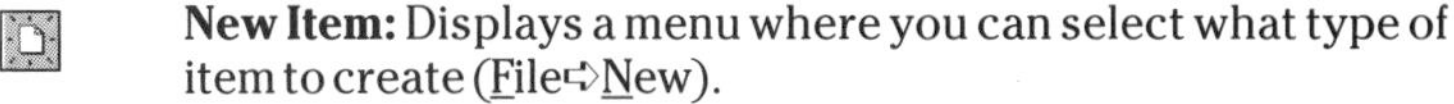

New Item: Displays a menu where you can select what type of item to create (File⇨New).

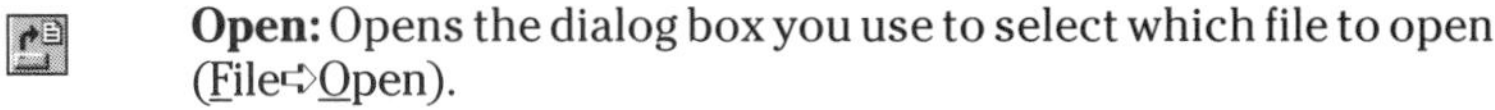

Open: Opens the dialog box you use to select which file to open (File⇨Open).

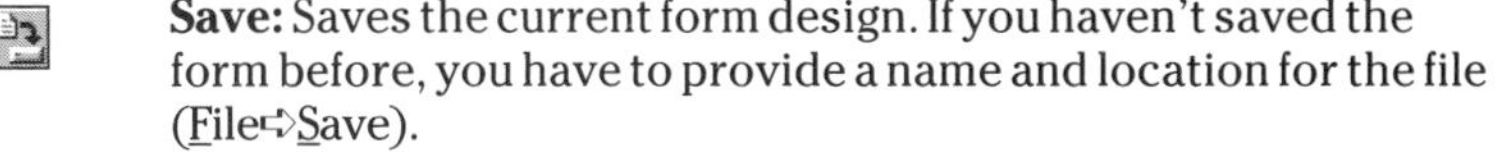

Save: Saves the current form design. If you haven't saved the form before, you have to provide a name and location for the file (File⇨Save).

Print: Opens the Print dialog box where you can make decisions about printing the form's design (File⇨Print).

Cut: Removes the selected text and puts it on the Clipboard (Edit⇨Cut).

Copy: Copies the selected text onto the Clipboard (Edit⇨Copy).

Paste: Inserts the contents of the Cipboard (Edit⇨Paste).

Use Form: Displays the current form so that you can work with it (View⇨Form).

Design Form: Opens the form in the Form Designer where you can make changes to the structure of the form. When you see this Speedbar, this button is depressed (View⇨Form Design).

Layout View: Switches to Layout view where you can make changes to how the controls look and function (View⇨Layout View).

Order View: Switches to Order view where you can make changes to the order in which you move between controls when using the form (View⇨Order View).

Order Control: Sets the order of the controls. Only available in Order view (View➪Order View).

Send to Back: Moves the selected item(s) as far from the viewer as possible so that other items appear on top of the selected item(s). Only available in Layout view (Layout➪Send to Back).

Bring to Front: Moves the selected item(s) to the front so that other items appear behind the selected item(s). Only available in Layout view (Layout➪Bring to Front).

Send Farther: Moves the selected item(s) back one layer. Only available in Layout view (Layout➪Send Farther).

Bring Closer: Moves the selected item(s) one layer closer to the viewer. Only available in Layout view (Layout➪Bring Closer).

Left Align: Aligns the left edge of the selected controls. Only available in Layout view (Layout➪Align Left).

Right Align: Aligns the right edge of the selected controls. Only available in Layout view (Layout➪Align Right).

Top Align: Aligns the tops of the selected controls. Only available in Layout view (Layout➪Align Top).

Bottom Align: Aligns the bottoms of the selected controls. Only available in Layout view (Layout➪Align Bottom).

Navigator: Opens the Navigator so that you can work with your items (Window➪1 Navigator).

Command window: Opens the Command window. You probably won't ever need to do this (Window➪2 Command).

Form Expert: Opens the Form Expert for creating a new form. The process of creating a new form is described in Catalog➪New Form (Help➪Experts).

Interactive Tutor: Displays the first screen of the Interactive Tutors where you can select a topic for dBASE to help you with (Help➪Interactive Tutors).

Form View SpeedBar

You get this SpeedBar when you are working with the records in a form. Forms are used either to enter information or to present the information in the records so that the information is easier to read and to edit. All of the commands on the Form menu are the same as those that appear on the Table menu when you are viewing a table. To conserve space, commands that appear on both menus are discussed under an entry for the Table menu (so Form⇨Add Records is under Table⇨Add Records).

New Item: Displays a menu where you can select what type of item to create (File⇨New).

Open: Opens the dialog box you use to select which file to open (File⇨Open).

Print: Opens the Print dialog box where you can make decisions about printing the form using records from the associated table or query (File⇨Print).

Cut: Removes the selected text and puts it on the Clipboard (Edit⇨Cut).

Copy: Copies the selected text onto the Clipboard (Edit⇨Copy).

Paste: Inserts the contents of the Clipboard (Edit⇨Paste).

Use Form: Displays the current form so that you can work with it. Because you have to be viewing the form to see this SpeedBar, this button must be depressed (View⇨Form).

Design Form: Opens the form in the Form Designer where you can make changes to the structure of the form (View⇨Form Design).

Find: Searches a selected field for any matches to the text you enter. (Although the command is Form⇨Find Records, it is discussed under Table⇨Find Records).

Add Records: Creates a blank copy of the form where you can enter new information. (Although the command is Form⇨Add Records, it is discussed under Table⇨Add Records).

First Record: Jumps you to the first record in the table associated with the form. dBASE refers to this record as the top record. (Although the command is Form⇨Top Record, it is discussed under Table⇨Top Record).

Previous Record: Moves to the previous record in the table. (Although the command is Form⇨Previous Record, it is discussed under Table⇨Previous Record).

Next Record: Moves to the next record in the table. (Although the command is Form⇨Next Record, it is discussed under Table⇨Next Record).

Last Record: Jumps to the last record in the table. dBASE refers to this record as the bottom record. (Although the command is Form⇨Bottom Record, it is discussed under Table⇨Bottom Record).

Navigator: Opens the Navigator so that you can work with your items (Window⇨1 Navigator).

Command window: Opens the Command window. You probably won't ever need to do this (Window⇨2 Command).

Form Expert: Opens the Form Expert for creating a new form. The process of creating a new form is described in Catalog⇨New Form (Help⇨Experts).

Interactive Tutor: Displays the first screen of the Interactive Tutors where you can select a topic for dBASE to help you with (Help⇨Interactive Tutors).

Image Viewer SpeedBar

In order to view an image that has been stored in a binary field within a table, you need to open the image. The easiest way to do this is to double-click on the image, although you can use View⇨Field Contents. When viewing an image, you get this SpeedBar.

New Item: Displays a menu where you can select what type of item to create (File⇨New).

Open: Opens the dialog box you use to select which file to open (File⇨Open).

Print: Opens the Print dialog box where you can make decisions about printing the image (File⇨Print).

Navigator: Opens the Navigator so that you can work with your items (Window⇨1 Navigator).

Command window: Opens the Command window. You probably won't ever need to do this (Window⇨2 Command).

Form Expert: Opens the Form Expert for creating a new form. The process of creating a new form is described in Catalog⇨New Form (Help⇨Experts).

Interactive Tutor: Displays the first screen of the Interactive Tutors where you can select a topic for dBASE to help you with (Help⇨Interactive Tutors).

Navigator SpeedBar

The Navigator lets you see all of the items available in the current directory and, if the search path is in use, along the search path. This SpeedBar is very similar to the Catalog Window SpeedBar, but there are a few items that can be displayed in the Navigator that cannot appear in a catalog (such as a catalog file or an image).

New Item: Displays a menu where you can select what type of item to create (File⇨New).

Open: Opens the dialog box you use to select which file to open (File⇨Open).

Cut: Removes the selected text and puts it on the Clipboard (Edit⇨Cut).

Copy: Copies the selected text onto the Clipboard (Edit⇨Copy).

Paste: Inserts the contents of the Clipboard (Edit⇨Paste).

Use Item: Opens the selected item for use (one of the Navigator⇨Run items such as Navigator⇨Run Form).

Design Item: Opens the selected item in its designer. For example, a report is opened in Crystal Reports, and a form is opened in the Form Designer (one of the Navigator⇨Design *item* commands such as Navigator⇨Design Form or, if you've selected an untitled item, one of the Navigator⇨New *item* commands such as Navigator⇨New Form.)

Delete: Removes the selected item from your disk. Be careful. Once you remove an item, it's very hard (if not impossible) to recover it. No matter what, you'll definitely have to bribe a guru to get it back (Edit⇨Delete).

Navigator: Opens the Navigator so that you can work with your items. Since you are in the Navigator SpeedBar when you see this button, this button must be depressed (Window⇨1 Navigator).

Command window: Opens the Command window. You probably won't ever need to do this (Window⇨2 Command).

Form Expert: Opens the Form Expert for creating a new form. The process of creating a new form is described in Catalog⇨New Form (Help⇨Experts).

Interactive Tutor: Displays the first screen of the Interactive Tutors where you can select a topic for dBASE to help you with (Help⇨Interactive Tutors).

OLE Viewer SpeedBar

An OLE field in dBASE can hold an OLE object, which is a document or part of a document that is managed by another program. When you are looking at a table in your database, dBASE displays an icon in the field to indicate that the field contains an OLE object. Of course, you need a way of viewing the actual object. You can either double-click on the object or select the object and select View⇨Field Contents. When you do, dBASE opens the OLE Viewer. From the OLE Viewer, you can decide whether to open the program that is actually managing the object.

New Item: Displays a menu where you can select what type of item to create (File⇨New).

Open: Opens the dialog box you use to select which file to open (File⇨Open).

Cut: Removes the selected text and puts it on the Clipboard (Edit⇨Cut).

Copy: Copies the selected text onto the Clipboard (Edit⇨Copy).

Paste: Inserts the contents of the Clipboard (Edit⇨Paste).

Activate: Causes the object to perform any associated action. With a sound, this plays a sound. With animation, this plays the animation. With text, this opens the managing program so that you can read the text in its native format. (The Activate Object topic is under Edit⇨Object.)

Edit: Opens the managing program so that you can make changes to the object. (The Open Object topic is under Edit⇨Object.)

Navigator: Opens the Navigator so that you can work with your items (Window⇨1 Navigator).

Command window: Opens the Command window. You probably won't ever need to do this (Window⇨2 Command).

Form Expert: Opens the Form Expert for creating a new form. The process of creating a new form is described in Catalog⇨New Form (Help⇨Experts).

Interactive Tutor: Displays the first screen of the Interactive Tutors where you can select a topic for dBASE to help you with (Help⇨Interactive Tutors).

Query Designer SpeedBar

When you are designing a question to ask of your database, you use the Query Designer and this SpeedBar.

New Item: Displays a menu where you can select what type of item to create (File⇨New).

Open: Opens the dialog box you use to select which file to open (File⇨Open).

Save: Saves the current query. If you haven't saved the query before, you have to provide a name and location for the file (File⇨Save).

Print: Opens the Print dialog box where you can make decisions about printing the query screen (File⇨Print).

Cut: Removes the selected text and puts it on the Clipboard (Edit⇨Cut).

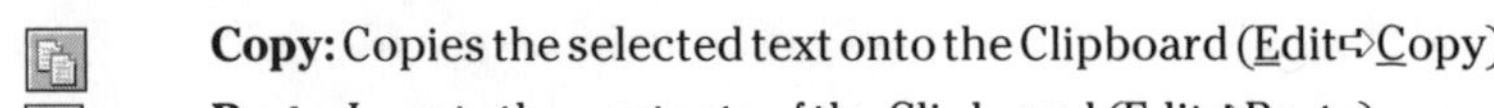

Copy: Copies the selected text onto the Clipboard (Edit⇨Copy).

Paste: Inserts the contents of the Clipboard (Edit⇨Paste).

Use Query: Displays the results of the current query so that you can work with it. When you are viewing a query, you actually use the Table Records SpeedBar (View⇨Query Results).

Design Query: Opens the form in the Query Designer where you can make changes to the question you are trying to ask. For information about creating a new query, see Catalog⇨New Query. This button must be depressed in order for you to see the Query Designer SpeedBar (View⇨Query Design).

Add Table: Opens a dialog box where you can select another table to add to the Query Designer screen (Query⇨Add Table).

Remove Table: Removes the selected table from the Query Designer screen (Query⇨Remove Selected Table).

Set Relation: Creates a relationship between two tables (Query⇨Set Relation).

Remove Relation: Removes the relationship between the current table and its parent (Query⇨Remove Relation).

Navigator: Opens the Navigator so that you can work with your items (Window⇨1 Navigator).

Command window: Opens the Command window. You probably won't ever need to do this (Window⇨2 Command).

Form Expert: Opens the Form Expert for creating a new form. The process of creating a new form is described in Catalog⇨New Form (Help⇨Experts).

Interactive Tutor: Displays the first screen of the Interactive Tutors where you can select a topic for dBASE to help you with (Help⇨Interactive Tutors).

Reports and Labels SpeedBar

You get the same SpeedBar whether you are viewing a standard report, a cross-tab, or a set of labels. Because all of these items are actually created in Crystal Reports, what you can do with them in dBASE is somewhat limited. Basically, you can either preview the file or print it. To make changes, you need to open the report or labels in Crystal Reports (for example, by using File⇨Open, Catalog⇨Design Report, or Navigator⇨Design Report for a report).

New Item: Displays a menu where you can select what type of item to create (File⇨New).

Open: Opens the dialog box you use to select which file to open (File⇨Open).

Print: Starts printing the report or labels (File⇨Print).

First Page: Jumps to the first page of the report or set of labels (Report⇨Top Page or Label⇨Top Page).

Previous Page: Moves to the previous page in the report or set of labels (Report⇨Previous Page or Label⇨Previous Page).

Next Page: Moves to the next page in the report or set of labels (Report⇨Next Page or Label⇨Next Page).

Last Page: Jumps to the last page of the report or set of labels (Report⇨Bottom Page or Label⇨Bottom Page).

Navigator: Opens the Navigator so that you can work with your items (Window⇨1 Navigator).

Command window: Opens the Command window. You probably won't ever need to do this (Window⇨2 Command).

Form Expert: Opens the Form Expert for creating a new form. The process of creating a new form is described in Catalog⇨New Form (Help⇨Experts).

Interactive Tutor: Displays the first screen of the Interactive Tutors where you can select a topic for dBASE to help you with (Help⇨Interactive Tutors).

Table Designer SpeedBar

When you are working with the structure of a table (as opposed to the contents of the table), you work in the Table Designer with this SpeedBar.

New Item: Displays a menu where you can select what type of item to create (File⇨New).

Open: Opens the dialog box you use to select which file to open (File⇨Open).

Save: Saves the current table structure. If you haven't saved the table before, you have to provide a name and location for the file (File⇨Save).

Print: Opens the Print dialog box where you can print a copy of the table's structure (File⇨Print).

Cut: Removes the selected text and puts it on the Clipboard (Edit⇨Cut).

Copy: Copies the selected text onto the Clipboard (Edit⇨Copy).

Paste: Inserts the contents of the Clipboard (Edit⇨Paste).

Use Table: Displays the contents of the current table so that you can work with the records (View⇨Table Records).

Design Table: Opens the Table Structure window where you can make changes to the structure of the table and the definitions of the fields. For information about creating a new query, see Catalog⇨New Table. This button must be depressed to see the Table Structure SpeedBar (View⇨Table Structure).

Add Field: Adds a new field definition line at the bottom of the table structure (Structure⇨Add Field).

Insert Field: Inserts a new field definition line above the current field definition (Structure⇨Insert Field).

Delete Field: Deletes the selected field definition(s) (Structure⇨Delete Selected Field).

Navigator: Opens the Navigator so that you can work with your items (Window⇨1 Navigator).

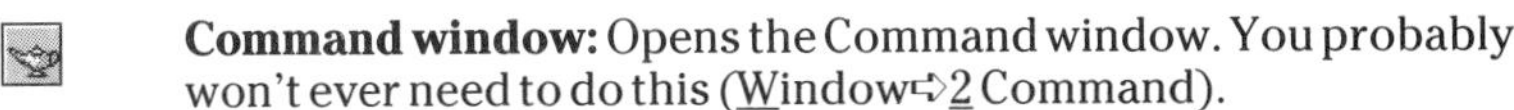

Command window: Opens the Command window. You probably won't ever need to do this (Window⇨2 Command).

Form Expert: Opens the Form Expert for creating a new form. The process of creating a new form is described in Catalog⇨New Form (Help⇨Experts).

Interactive Tutor: Displays the first screen of the Interactive Tutors where you can select a topic for dBASE to help you with (Help⇨Interactive Tutors).

Table Records Window SpeedBar

New Item: Displays a menu where you can select what type of item to create (File⇨New).

Open: Opens the dialog box you use to select which file to open (File⇨Open).

Save: Saves the current record. Actually, this command isn't necessary, but it's there if you want it (File⇨Save Record).

Print: Opens the Print dialog box where you can make decisions about records from the table (File⇨Print).

Cut: Removes the selected text and puts it on the Clipboard (Edit⇨Cut).

Copy: Copies the selected text onto the Clipboard (Edit⇨Copy).

Paste: Inserts the contents of the Clipboard (Edit⇨Paste).

Use Table: Displays the contents of the current table so that you can work with the records. This button must be depressed to see this SpeedBar (View⇨Table Records).

Design Query: Opens the Table Structure window where you can make changes to the structure of the table and the definitions of the fields (View⇨Table Structure).

Browse View: Switches to displaying the records as rows and the fields as columns. With this view, you can see more than one record at a time (View⇨Browse Layout).

Form View: Switches to displaying a single record on the screen with the fields arranged across the screen (View⇨Form Layout).

Column View: Switches to displaying a single record with each field in its own row (View⇨Columnar Layout).

Find: Searches a selected field for any matches to the text you enter (Table⇨Find Records).

Add Records: Creates a blank copy of the form where you can enter new information (Table⇨Add Records).

New Query: Creates a new query. This moves you to the Query Designer (Table⇨Create Query).

First Record: Jumps you to the first record in the table associated with the form. dBASE refers to this record as the top record (Table⇨Top Record).

Previous Screen: Moves back to the previous screen of records (Table⇨Previous Page).

Previous Record: Moves to the previous record in the table (Table⇨Previous Record).

Next Record: Moves to the next record in the table (Table⇨Next Record).

Next Screen: Moves to the next screen of records (Table⇨Next Page).

Last Record: Jumps to the last record in the table. dBASE refers to this record as the bottom record (Table⇨Bottom Record).

Navigator: Opens the Navigator so that you can work with your items (Window⇨1 Navigator).

Command window: Opens the Command window. You probably won't ever need to do this (Window⇨2 Command).

Form Expert: Opens the Form Expert for creating a new form. The process of creating a new form is described in Catalog⇨New Form (Help⇨Experts).

Interactive Tutor: Displays the first screen of the Interactive Tutors where you can select a topic for dBASE to help you with (Help⇨Interactive Tutors).

Text Editor SpeedBar

The Text Editor is used both for working with dBASE programs (a topic I won't get into) and with the contents of memo fields. The contents of a memo field are represented by an icon within your table; to view the actual contents, you need to either double-click on the icon or select the icon and select View⇨Field Contents. When you do, the contents of the memo field are displayed within the Text Editor with this SpeedBar. There are additional buttons listed below that only appear on the SpeedBar when you are working with a program.

New Item: Displays a menu where you can select what type of item to create (File⇨New).

Open: Opens the dialog box you use to select which file to open (File⇨Open).

Save: Saves the text in the field (File⇨Save).

Print: Opens the Print dialog box where you can make decisions about printing the text (File⇨Print).

Cut: Removes the selected text and puts it on the Clipboard (Edit⇨Cut).

Copy: Copies the selected text onto the Clipboard (Edit⇨Copy).

Paste: Inserts the contents of the Clipboard (Edit⇨Paste).

Find Text: Searches for matching text within the current memo field or program (Edit⇨Search⇨Find Text).

Replace Text: Finds matching text and replaces it with the new text you specify (Edit⇨Search⇨Replace Text).

Navigator: Opens the Navigator so that you can work with your items (Window⇨1 Navigator).

Command window: Opens the Command window. You probably won't ever need to do this (Window⇨2 Command).

Form Expert: Opens the Form Expert for creating a new form. The process of creating a new form is described in Catalog⇨New Form (Help⇨Experts).

Interactive Tutor: Displays the first screen of the Interactive Tutors where you can select a topic for dBASE to help you with (Help⇨Interactive Tutors).

Glossary

bands

Groups of former dBASE for DOS programmers often form into *bands*. Actually, the various sections of a Crystal Reports screen are called bands or group sections. Each and every record prints in the Details band, and each group has both a header band and a footer band. For more information on creating bands in a report, see CatalogÍNew Report.

binary

The counting system based on counting on your hands (2) rather than your fingers (10). In dBASE, it refers to a type of field that can contain either images or sounds.

builder

A dialog box that is designed to help you fill in another dialog box. You can tell when a builder is available by looking for a button at the end of a box you are trying to complete. If the button has a little wrench icon on it, then clicking on it probably opens a builder. There's a color builder for selecting the colors on a form, and there's the most important builder of all: the Expression Builder (discussed under EditÍBuild Expression).

calculated field

A field that dBASE fills in for you using values from other fields. For example, you may calculate the total cost of a purchase by multiplying the value of the QUANTITY field by the value of the PRICE field. Whenever possible, you should create a calculated field with an expression and make dBASE do the work for you.

catalog

Well, *Victoria's Secret* is probably the best known, but *Lillian Vernon* is also a contender. Very different catalogs. In dBASE, you use a catalog to organize all the items related to a single project. A catalog can contain a collection of database tables, forms, queries, reports, and labels. You may want one catalog for the files associated with your customer mailing list and another for the employees in the company. The same item (such as a report or set of labels) may be in both catalogs.

child table

A table that contains records related to another table by a special linking field. If things are set up properly, all the records in the child table have one and only one record in the parent table that they are related to. (Obviously, no one at Borland ever studied biology.)

Clipboard

The place where Windows stores information that you have cut or copied from your document. When you select Edit⇨Paste, the information from the Clipboard is inserted into your document. Unlike the little people in the printer who carry buckets of ink and quill pens to print your documents, the inhabitants of the Clipboard all carry little notebooks and pencils because the information in the Clipboard is replaced every time you cut or copy something new.

condition

Something you should see your doctor about, or part of a question in a query. When you create a query, you ask dBASE to check each record against some rule that you have created. For example, you may ask dBASE to check if the AGE field contains a value greater than 21. That rule (>21) is the condition. Conditions are often used as part of expressions.

control

What I lose toward the end of each and every book project. In dBASE, anything that you place on a form is called a control. More realistically, a control is an object on the form that lets you control what goes into a field.

cross-tab

A special type of report that focuses on the values in a single field and organizes the values into various groups and subgroups (represented by the rows and columns of the report). Standard reports only organize information into rows. To see a sample of a cross-tab, look at the entry for Catalog⇨New Cross-Tab.

Crystal Reports

The program that you actually use to create your reports from dBASE. This is a separate program, not developed by Borland, that is included in dBASE.

data

A character on one of my favorite (recently retired) television shows. Well, to tell you the truth, I use the term to mean the stuff that you put into your database. Computer science instructors who are reading from their textbooks will tell you that data is the collection of facts before it's been organized, and information is what you get after you organize. So, if you print an attractive, organized report listing all the stuff in your database, that's information. If you drop it down the stairs and the pages get all messed up, it's back to being data.

database

A tool for organizing a bunch of data into usable information. dBASE is probably the best-known database for microcomputers.

data type

The part of a field description that tells dBASE what type of data to expect. Each data type is stored differently, so it's important that dBASE be able to tell the different types apart. Some of the common data types are character, numeric, date, binary (for pictures or sounds), OLE (for objects managed by other programs), and memo (for large amounts of text).

delimited file

A file where the fields are separated by a special character, often a comma (as in a Comma Delimited File). The special character marks the end (or "de limit") of each field.

editor (as in text, program, procedure)

Notice the phrase *(as in text, program, procedure)*—that's so I don't get to make any comments about the editors who work on my books. Oh, well, that's what the acknowledgments are for, anyway. In dBASE, an editor is a little program that allows you to make changes to the text within a memo field or a program. (A procedure is a part of a program.) All the commands for the Text Editor (which is what you use with either a program or a memo field) are covered in the Command Reference.

embed

After writing for several hours, you may find the mouse *embedded* in your hand. OK, the real description is that an *embedded* object is an object that is actually managed by another program but created and stored entirely within dBASE. In contrast, a *linked* object is created and managed by another program and exists as a separate file outside of dBASE (even after being inserted). Both types of objects are actually created, edited, and usually displayed by the other program. The difference is that an embedded object doesn't exist as a separate file. Embed is what you do to an object to make it embedded. All of this is part of the magic of OLE.

expression

Shucky darn has always been one of my favorite expressions. In dBASE, expressions are much more boring; they are simply instructions to dBASE to perform a specific task (see *scope expression)*. Mathematical expressions are used to calculate values for reports, for calculated fields, or for use in other expressions. A math expression can include values from fields, values within the expression, and standard mathematical operators (like +, -, *, and /) as well as functions. A math expression can be solved for an answer. A logical expression usually compares the value of a field to a condition (AGE <= 65) and can be used to select records.

field

A big, grassy area where people go for picnics and to play. Also, a category of information in a database (but not for playing). A field is the container that holds the stuff you put into your database. The LAST NAME field can contain anyone's last name. Actually, you can probably put anything you want into the field, but because it's called Last Name, people are going to assume that what's in there really is a last name of someone. The only way to control what's in a field is by restricting the contents to a *data type* (see that entry for more info) or by using a *validation rule* (something that's way beyond this reference). When you're viewing records in the Browse Layout view, a field is a single column containing information.

field name

The name used for referring to a field. What's inside the field doesn't really have to match the field name. When you're viewing records in the Browse Layout view, a field name is the text in the gray box at the top of the column.

field type

Same as data type. Well, OK, there's a slight difference. A field type describes what type of information the field expects, and the data type is what type of information the data actually is. You put the data into the field.

For

One of the two most important scope expressions. A For expression selects records that make the expression true. For example, if you enter **PRICE < 1** in the For box, the expression selects only those records where the value in the field PRICE is less than 1. You can make the expression as complex or as simple as you want, using any or all of the fields within the table or query.

form

Organizes the fields from the record so that they are easier to read and use; usually used for displaying information on-screen. Very often, there are separate forms for entering data and for using the information. A single form generally displays only one record. The only exception is a form that displays a single parent record and all the child records for that parent. You can print a form, but each record prints as a separate image (usually on a separate sheet of paper).

format

How something is organized or displayed. With dBASE, you can have formats that cause all the text in a field to be displayed as uppercase or that display a number with a dollar sign and two decimals. In Crystal Reports, you can also format fields so that they're bold or italic. Within forms, you can even change the color of the various parts to create some amazingly ugly displays.

index

The part of the book that follows the glossary. In dBASE, an index is used to make it easier to find a value within a field. For a much more detailed (and much more boring) definition, see Table⇨Table Utilities⇨Manage Indexes.

link

A character from the old *Mod Squad* show (boy, am I getting old). In Windows, a link is one of two ways in which an object can be inserted into a file (the other is *embed).* You can link an object stored in a separate file to an OLE field within dBASE. The contents of the file appear within the field but are actually managed by the program that originally created the file. Also, in dBASE, programmers talk about the link between the parent record and the child record; more often, the linking field is the field that is shared between the parent record and the child record.

linking field

The field that is common between a parent table and a child table.

locking

Only used on systems where several people can use the same database at the same time; reserves the current record so that only the current user can make changes to it. If you lock the record, only you can make changes. If someone else locks it, you can't make any changes to that record until the other person unlocks it.

menu

A list of choices. In Windows, the menu names are listed across the top of the screen on the menu bar. You can click a menu name to see that menu (or you can press the Alt key followed by the underlined letter from the menu name). In a restaurant, the salad bar is listed on the menu.

Navigator

The control center for dBASE; lists all the dBASE files that it can find. It always looks in the current directory and can be set to check other directories by using a search path. Although the Navigator is useful for finding dBASE files, an easier way to work with your files is to organize them into catalogs.

object

Something in your database that can be worked with as a whole thing. In some cases, a single object can be broken down into smaller objects. One type of object (which can't be broken down by dBASE) is the contents of OLE fields (which dBASE can only display); you need the program that is managing the object to make changes. The contents of fields are in some ways objects — some commands do things to the entire field rather than the contents. Controls on a form are another type of object and, in fact, have properties, which you can see by selecting a control using View⇨Object Properties.

OLE

Something a bullfighter yells. In Windows, it used to stand for Object Linking and Embedding, but Microsoft says it doesn't anymore. It now refers to a technique for combining things created in different programs. When it works, it's really cool. When it doesn't, it's a disaster.

Here's how it's supposed to work. Imagine that your computer has a program for creating animation complete with soundtrack. You decide that it would be neat to put little samples of that animation (including the nifty sounds) into your database or even a word processing document. Well, neither your word processor nor your database has the tools necessary for playing back the animation and sounds. Even worse, you may want to be able to edit the recordings after you put them into your database. So you need to have a way of putting the recording in your document while still letting your animation and sound programs manage it.

That's OLE! It lets you put the recording into your document (as an OLE object) and keeps track of which program should be used to play it back or to make changes. You have a choice between embedding the object (so that it only exists within the database) or linking it (which means it also exists as a file on your computer).

operator

Someone who tries to sell you waterfront property in the Everglades. In working with computer programs, you meet two common types of operators: mathematical and logical. The mathematical operators are the ones you learned in elementary school: add (+), subtract (-), multiply (*), and divide (/). The logical operators are used to compare things, and you probably didn't learn them until junior high. They are equal (=), less than (<), greater than (>), and their opposites (<> for not equal, >= for greater than or equal to, and <= for less than or equal to).

parent table

A parent table contains records that share a common field with another table (called a child table). The common field is often referred to as the *linking field*. Each parent record has a different value in the common field — but a record in a child table may have the same value in the common field as a parent table. Any number of child table records may have the same value in the common field. A single parent record may have no children, one child, or several children.

programming

Writing cryptic instructions that only your computer can understand. When you create a program, your computer can do the task described by the program without your having to be involved. This is a very nerdy activity for which some people make lots and lots of money. The rest of us just write books.

properties

The characteristics of an object. In dBASE, these considerations are most important when designing forms where each control has properties that determine the color of the control, its size and position, and even what it says.

query

A set of questions for your database. You create a query using the Query Designer screen and by writing conditions for the various fields in the query. For more about creating your own queries, see Catalog⇨New Query.

record

What your lawyer hopes you don't have if someone is building a case against you. The more boring definition: the entries for a single individual or item in a table. When you're looking at your data in Browse view, a record is a single row. When you are using Form or Columnar view, each record is displayed individually on-screen.

relation

Someone who can show up at your door and expect a room for a week or two. In dBASE, just like in real life, the most important relation is between the child and parent. The difference is that in dBASE the relation is between records in the child table and the parent table.

report

A summary of the information in your database, usually printed. A report organizes the records, groups them into related sections, performs calculations, and presents the whole thing in an attractive format. In dBASE, you use a separate program, Crystal Reports, to write your reports.

scope expression

An expression used to select records for printing, deleting, or any number of other activ-ities. The options for a scope expres-sion include All (all the records are checked), Rest (dBASE starts with the current record and moves toward the end of the table), Next (you enter a number and dBASE looks at only that many re-cords), and Record (dBASE looks only at that single record).

You can also add either a For or a While expression to have dBASE select only certain records out of the group it's looking at. After reading the current record, dBASE first uses the While expression to determine whether to bother looking at any more records. If the expression for the While is no longer true, then dBASE stops. It then checks which of the selection options is marked (All, Next, Rest, or Record) to determine whether the current record is included. If not (for example, you requested the next ten, and this is the eleventh record), then dBASE stops. Finally, dBASE checks to see whether the values in the record make the expression in the For box true. If not, then dBASE moves on to the next record. If the record is approved (it makes the For expression true), then dBASE uses the record for whatever task is being controlled by the scope expression.

scroll bars

The bars at the right edge and bottom of a window that let you move around within your document or program. Each window may be showing only part of the whole picture. You use the scroll bars to change what's showing in the window. If you need help with using scroll bars, check out *Windows For Dummies* (also published by IDG Books Worldwide).

SDF file

Stands for *System Data File,* which is a fancy Borland term for a file in which a field is always the same length, no matter what it contains. For example, the FIRST NAME field may be 15 columns wide. If your first name only has six characters, the remaining nine columns are filled with spaces to make your first name 15 columns wide.

search path

A list of directories that dBASE checks for files to list in the Navigator. You activate the search path by using the Properties⇨Desktop command.

section

A portion of a report. Most reports have a Details section where each and every record in the report is printed. Around the Details section may be group sections, which are only printed whenever a new group starts. A group header section appears before the details for that group, and a group footer appears after the details. For an example, see Catalog⇨New Report.

session

Each time you open a new table or query in dBASE, you create a separate session. Each session can have its own property settings, meaning that how things work for that table may be different than for other tables you have opened. To eliminate sessions (so that all of your tables are controlled by the same property settings), use the Sessions option in the Files category under Properties⇨Desktop.

sort

Puts the contents of a table or window in order. You can use an Index to sort the records within your table, or you can create a new, sorted table by using Table⇨Table Utilities⇨Sort Records.

SpeedBar

Everybody else in the world calls these things *toolbars*, but not Borland. A SpeedBar appears at the top of the screen (right below the menu bar) and contains buttons that activate various commands. For a description of most of the dBASE SpeedBars, see Stuart's Superior SpeedBar Survey (the section right before this one).

SpeedMenu

One of the very useful menus that appear when you click the right mouse button (by "right mouse button," I mean the mouse button on the right, as opposed to the correct mouse button, which could be either the left or the right button or even the one in the middle). SpeedMenus are available when you are performing most — but not all — tasks. The best way to learn to use them is by constantly clicking the right button to see what happens.

summary value

In a cross-tab, the value that the whole report is designed to summarize. In a standard report, it can be the values in any field that are summarized when the group changes.

table

The actual item that contains the information in your database. A table is made up of fields and filled with records. Two tables may be related as a parent table and a child table. Each table is described by its table structure.

table structure

The description of the fields that make up a table. Each field is described in terms of its data type, its length (if appropriate), whether it has a decimal point and, if so, how many values follow the decimal (for numeric fields), and whether the field is indexed. The table structure is what holds the information in the table. Changing the table structure changes what the table can hold. In some cases, if you make a drastic change, the table will no longer be able to hold the information that was in it, and you may lose some of your data.

template

A code used to format the values from a field. dBASE has a wide variety of templates, including ones to make all the letters in a field uppercase, to control the placement of the currency symbol, to control the display of zeros, and to insert special characters.

value

The contents of a field. The value is the actual data that is put into your database. You can also use a value in an expression, where the value is anything you type (such as a number or a word).

viewer

A tool for viewing the contents of certain types of fields. You need a viewer to work with the contents of text fields (the Text Editor), binary fields (either the Image Viewer or the Sound Player), and OLE fields (the OLE Viewer). Each viewer has its own set of menu commands, which you use to make changes to the field contents. These commands are described in the Command Reference.

While

The part of a scope expression that controls how long dBASE keeps checking records. Generally, the expression compares a field's contents with a value (something like STATE = "WA"). If the While expression is not true for the current record, then dBASE doesn't bother to look at anything else. If the first record has a value that makes the expression true, dBASE continues looking at records until it finds one that makes the expression false. At that point, it stops looking.

z-ordering

The order of the layers on a form. Each control has its own layer. When you move between controls, you are actually moving between layers. Controls on layers in the front (with a higher z-order) can cover up controls on other layers (with a lower z-order). The layer at the far back always has a z-order value of 1.

Index

IDG BOOKS WORLDWIDE REGISTRATION CARD

RETURN THIS REGISTRATION CARD FOR FREE CATALOG

Title of this book: DBASE 5 FOR WINDOWS FOR DUMMIES QR

My overall rating of this book: ❑ Very good [1] ❑ Good [2] ❑ Satisfactory [3] ❑ Fair [4] ❑ Poor [5]

How I first heard about this book:

❑ Found in bookstore; name: [6]

❑ Book review: [7]

❑ Advertisement: [8]

❑ Catalog: [9]

❑ Word of mouth; heard about book from friend, co-worker, etc.: [10]

❑ Other: [11]

What I liked most about this book:

What I would change, add, delete, etc., in future editions of this book:

Other comments:

Number of computer books I purchase in a year: ❑ 1 [12] ❑ 2-5 [13] ❑ 6-10 [14] ❑ More than 10 [15]

I would characterize my computer skills as: ❑ Beginner [16] ❑ Intermediate [17] ❑ Advanced [18] ❑ Professional [19]

I use ❑ DOS [20] ❑ Windows [21] ❑ OS/2 [22] ❑ Unix [23] ❑ Macintosh [24] ❑ Other: [25] ____________ (please specify)

I would be interested in new books on the following subjects:
(please check all that apply, and use the spaces provided to identify specific software)

❑ Word processing: [26]

❑ Spreadsheets: [27]

❑ Data bases: [28]

❑ Desktop publishing: [29]

❑ File Utilities: [30]

❑ Money management: [31]

❑ Networking: [32]

❑ Programming languages: [33]

❑ Other: [34]

I use a PC at (please check all that apply): ❑ home [35] ❑ work [36] ❑ school [37] ❑ other: [38] ____________

The disks I prefer to use are ❑ 5.25 [39] ❑ 3.5 [40] ❑ other: [41] ____________

I have a CD ROM: ❑ yes [42] ❑ no [43]

I plan to buy or upgrade computer hardware this year: ❑ yes [44] ❑ no [45]

I plan to buy or upgrade computer software this year: ❑ yes [46] ❑ no [47]

Name:

Business title: [48]

Type of Business: [49]

Address (❑ home [50] ❑ work [51]/Company name:)

Street/Suite#

City [52]/State [53]/Zipcode [54]:

Country [55]

❑ **I liked this book!**
You may quote me by name in future IDG Books Worldwide promotional materials.

My daytime phone number is ____________

IDG BOOKS

THE WORLD OF COMPUTER KNOWLEDGE

Please keep me informed about IDG's World of Computer Knowledge. Send me the latest IDG Books catalog.

NO POSTAGE
NECESSARY
IF MAILED
IN THE
UNITED STATES

BUSINESS REPLY MAIL

FIRST CLASS MAIL PERMIT NO. 2605 SAN MATEO, CALIFORNIA

IDG Books Worldwide
155 Bovet Rd
San Mateo CA 94402-9833

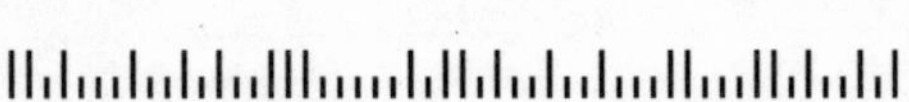